Mouse-ear
Chickweed

Knapweed

Wild Oat

Samphire

Cornflower

Common Red Poppy

Hare's Foot Trefoil

Yellow

Cowslip

Mouse Tail

Wild Flowers for the Garden

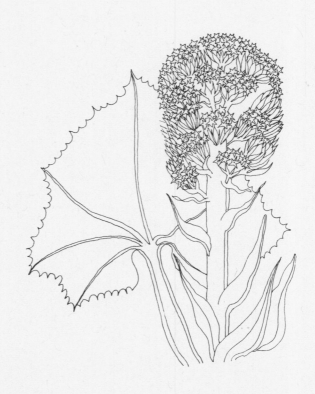

Wild Flowers for the Garden

Stephen Dealler

Drawings by Anne Baikie

B.T.Batsford Ltd, London

First published 1977
© Stephen Dealler 1977
ISBN 0 7134 0089 7 (cased)
ISBN 0 7134 0090 0 (limp)

Filmset in 12/13 pt. Monophoto Bembo by
Servis Filmsetting Ltd, Manchester
Printed in Great Britain by
The Anchor Press Ltd, Tiptree, Essex
for the publishers B.T.Batsford Ltd,
4 Fitzhardinge Street, London W1H 0AH

Foreword

by Peter Hardy MP,
author of the 'Conservation of Wild Creatures and Wild Plants Act 1975'.

I was delighted to learn of Stephen Dealler's book. It can serve a worthwhile purpose.

During 1975 I was fortunate enough to see my Private Member's Bill become law. For some years a Bill to protect the most endangered of our rare wild plants had existed but it had never come within sight of enactment. My first place in the ballot for Bills gave the necessary opportunity and I decided to present an amalgamation of that Bill and of a similar one in respect of rare wild creatures. The measure is timely and, I believe, offers the greater consistency in our arrangements which had become essential.

It is not unfitting that Mr Dealler, an Aberdonian, should write this book for several of the wild plants listed in the Act are to be found in Scotland, perhaps more of the rare plants are to be found nearer Mr Dealler's home than my own in South Yorkshire.

Further, it would be right to emphasize that Scotland possesses a rich variety of wild flora and that concern for British Natural History is by no means restricted to the south of my own country.

That there is widespread concern is beyond dispute and through this interest there has been encouragement for the efforts of those of us who wish to ensure that the conservation of our natural heritage is enhanced.

It is true that Members of Parliament with interests in this field are sometimes bombarded with peremptory and ill-informed demand for particular action. One can often sympathize with the concern whilst regretting the misapprehension. Mr Dealler's work may go some way to provide a remedy for that as well as making a substantial contribution to promoting both information and enthusiasm and this additional asset for the bookshelves of the lovers of Britain's nature should be much welcomed.

P. Hardy
PETER HARDY MP
HOUSE OF COMMONS
DECEMBER 1976.

'Is it not,' says *Mr Curtis,* *'that we are too apt to treat with neglect the beautiful flowers of our own country because they are common and easily obtained?'*

THE LONDON FLORIST, 1815

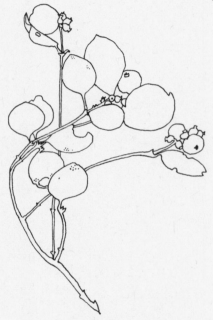

Contents

Acknowledgments

This book grew from the thoughts and lessons of many gardeners. I hardly know how to thank them all for the time and help they have given me over the past two years in bringing this book from idea to reality, special thanks must go to the staffs of the Kew and Royal Horticultural Society libraries along with those of all the British and French libraries in which I have researched.

I must thank the many people who lent me illustrative material: Mr Henrickson, Mr Young, Miss J. Merchant, Miss A. Summervill, and Bob Smith, all of whom are from Aberdeen. Thanks must also go to Andy Lucas and Alan Forster for expert photographic help.

The marvellous cover is by Gillian Condy and the illustrations are a result of much hard work by a talented Aberdeen Art School graduate, Anne Baikie. To both of them I extend my thanks.

For the foreword by Peter Hardy M.P., enthusiasm from David Bellamy encouragement and help from Mike Stephenson, time and energy from John Kelcey of the Botanical Society of Great Britain, thanks to all, but also and especially to the lads in my flat who have had to put up with a typewriter clattering away night and day to allow wild flowers to make a comeback.

STEPHEN DEALLER,
ABERDEEN 1976

List of Illustrations

(the figure in brackets indicates the relationship of the drawing to the natural size of the plant)

An Introduction

Wild is a word often associated with bad temper, with disorganization and violence; it is also prefixed to flowers and this betrays, I believe, the general feeling that these plants have an independent mind of their own and do not react to man's touch. It would be such a pity if merely the word itself stopped us thinking of them as predictable and friendly, for few other words could deny the hidden order of the natural plant habitat so completely.

Within apparent wildness there is a regularity that is easy to display. How many times have you seen poppies climbing up trees, Policeman's Helmet in a desert or 7cm apple trees? Never! Each of those plants, and everyone knows it, has its own particular place in nature, and sticks to it. When you see a poppy in a cornfield it is as natural as it is expected and it is this inherent consistency that many people never really notice; it's just taken for granted.

Yet, it must be admitted, despite all the scientific order there is still that element of good old chaos which keeps us all interested, a modicum of chance which means we are not sure that a field will have poppies in it but how nice it is when it does. What looks wild and random from the layman's point of view is as scientifically predictable as horticulture is for the botanist. Yet we have two categories: wild flowers hidden away and known only to botanical boffins, hidden among woods and pastures and 'cultivated' garden flowers that may be only feet away inside the hedge, both categories with much the same characteristics. The advertising executive in me would like to call them 'free' and 'captive' flowers as the difference is purely semantic and, perhaps, with the help of this book, may decrease: They are only 'wild' because they're not in a garden. At one time wild flowers were garden flowers, though even Granny doesn't pretend to remember it, and before that there were no flower gardens at all, the pleasure from blooms came wild, straight from the ground. At one time no one even knew what seeds were for.

If one looks back into the history of gardening it will become apparent that it was not 'complex' in the modern sense of the word because for most of the past the only reasons for cultivation were nutritional, medicinal and religious. It was only in the fifteenth century, in England at least, that the idea of growing flowers for their purely aesthetic appeal became accepted practice. Mayster Ion Gardener, who was gardener to the King, wrote a poem (about 1445) which tells of those flowers he grew together with the herbs and vegetables (which, by the way, take up most of the ode). Those flowers were all, as far as the translators can tell, British national wild flowers which he took over and grew in his garden.

It is such a shame that the snobbery of the following centuries caused the favouring of those species that came from overseas and those which had been artificially produced.

In the early 1600s in the gardens of the gentry the primrose was grown in abundance. Red primroses! Though even now they are just not hardy at all. Blue primroses! Though they had great difficulty in propagating them. Polyanthus! (cowslip/primrose crosses) with varying eye colour; they all reached high prices among florists. There was already a concensus of what a good polyanthus should look like (exactly the right shape, height, colour etc.) and they had to conform only to the eye. Poppies were probably brought to Britain with the Romans when they were cultivated for their medicinal purposes and, as a sort of ritual indicator that corn crops were doing well, but since then they have been taken up as a candidate for merely visual improvement. Imported species *P. orientale* and *P. bracteum* were crossed in the eighteenth century to produce various colours, doubles, trebles, etc. most of which would revert to the natural species in time, and yet still no one has bothered to train the poppy to keep its petals longer. We have, however, come a long way in the breeding of the flowers that haunt our gardens; in fact for many years there have been societies which have the express aim of improving the species and making them hardier and more beautiful for our use. When this process reaches a certain stage it becomes something of a problem. Reading through the copies of the Year Book of one of these groups it becomes clear that there is continuous 'progress' in breeding, yet knowing where the process leads is only looked at speculatively. By careful gleaning, however, there appear to be character-istics – that a good daffodil (in this case), should have: flat petals, a large bowl, dry sepals that fall off early and do not change colour after opening, a wide cup; it should hold its head up and, most of all, it should win shows. Some of those things perhaps the gardener would appreciate as marks of beauty but, in reality, these attributes are demanded by legislating in a world of their own making as to what is beautiful and what is not. Roses and chrysanthemums, of course, suffer from the same intensive specializa-tion. Let us try to bring a little fresh air to the argument and realize that there is nothing particularly more beautiful about giant daffodils in com-parison with wild types.

The more complicated and specialized a culture becomes the further it strays from its inborn and 'natural' characteristics and, although 'woe and thrice woe' are not intended in this paragraph, the collapse of culture has often been attributed to over specialization. And it is increasingly in this direction breeders are going – further and further away from the ancient and common ideas of beauty and, in its place, cultivate the exotic, the forced, the 'unnatural' hybrid.

The issue is then, what constitutes natural, unforced beauty in plants?

Of course, no one can say for certain but the ideas on the subject seem to centre on and involve the unconcious, the intuitive. Intuitively, we know, all animals pass on information to their young on how to eat, sleep, grow, reproduce. Moving up the genetic scale, we find that less and less is passed intuitively but that man himself confers much on his offsprings to get them through their first few years and to make them behave like their parents. When the pianist hits the right chord it makes us sad or happy or jovial and the rhyme and reason behind this lies with our ancestors. Wild flowers mattered to our forebears so they ARE beautiful; when one is seen the old rusty hinges of memory's megalithic door creak open and we experience a bit of history, as pleasure.

One cannot understand the cultural gap between the 'natural' sense of the beautiful and our modern 'cultivated' sense unless one looks, albeit briefly, at the history of agriculture and man's attempt to control and tame flowers and plants in order to make them serve him.

The whole process is really one of jerks and bumps ever since man first found out that he could actually influence the growth of plants with seeds, techniques, i.e. his intelligence; whereupon he started to clear space for his own crops. At first this was generally at the upland level because it was easier to clear trees away, but eventually, under the influence of the Angles and the Saxons, the lower valleys were cultivated because they gave much higher yields and the population increased apace with the increase in the arable area. By the fourteenth century the population would have been around 13 million and the arable area really quite large, leaving probably half the country still as forest. This must have been an excellent age for flowers because of the huge new areas and niches they could fill (at this time it was considered normal that one seed planted in ten would be a weed). Then there came the great Black Death and with it a fall in the population of the country resulting in an actual surplus of usable land and a shortage of labour, but after a few hundred years, despite plagues and pestilences the population had increased enough to allow the process of deforestation to continue.

The Agrarian Revolution was almost achieved by Act of Parliament. Crop rotation, plant breeding, marling; the Corn Laws allowing the influx of cheap grain; the Enclosure Acts dividing up the rural population into landed gentry and a landless peasant class; tithe redemption; all of this served to force upon agriculture a much more efficient system. Much surplus food had to be produced, which meant small farms could not pay their way, small fields could not accommodate the machines that were needed, spare land was cleared and used as arable, and it all meant that the area of uncultivated land dropped drastically.

By the end of the eighteenth century the country had progressed as far as the technology would allow it and the surplus population drifted off to the towns, which thereupon grew and again cut down the common land around them. With accelerations during the two world wars the process of urbanization and farm mechanization has been going on ever since.

Now for the frightening statistics. Out of a total of about 50 million acres in the country, the ploughed acres reached a maximum in 1869 of 15.3 million; in 1915 10.97 million; in 1938 8.9 million; and in 1965 14.13 million. Other improved land reached a maximum in 1891 of 28.09 million and in 1935 25 million; in 1946 24.3 million; and in 1965 24.35 million.

To the layman, at first glance, this may show that the area of used land has dropped only slightly since the middle of the last century but really this is because of continued deforestation and since that time there have been enormous cuts in the size of our Royal forests. It all comes down to a massive movement of land from agricultural use into urban use and from disused waste to agriculture. From the five acres we each had in the 1500s we are now down to one acre; garden size has been reduced so that it can now no longer supply the food of the household but give only aesthetic pleasure and a few herbs. It must be said also Britain is one of the most urbanized countries in Europe with over 95 per cent of our people living in towns. Our farm sizes are huge compared to the Bavarian peasant with ten acres or the Southern French peasants with 12 acres. Yes, in this over-crowded island we have been pushed into the towns as agriculture takes up as much land as possible, and the countryside and the wilds disappear. It has left us with a little patch of grass to be tamed and cajoled into supplying all the things that the ancient pasture, wood, forest, heath, moor, swamp and hedge gave our ancestors. Is it possible? Can it supply all that lost green-ery? Green is the colour that the eye sees least (there are more green cars than any other colour but would you have said so?), but which, to quote the psychologists again, has genuine therapeutic uses in calming the mind; perhaps to primeval man it meant that there was food to be had. But let us not lose hope, with the right occupants, and the free rhythm of nature the garden can go some way to replacing our need for the spirit of the wilderness.

Common land has dwindled in the time since the Enclosure Acts; fen land has gone through an increased rate of drainage; mountain and upland areas receive grants to keep them in business; woodland has been removed; dry spots are irrigated and wet ones drained, clay soils are made lighter and lime ones more acid. That varied environment our ancestors knew has been replaced by a much more ecologically monolithic system where one correct habitat for a particular plant means other plants are dying out as a result! A place, where, as demanded by modern crops, farming methods and the drive for greater productivity, the acres are being standardized, and the old wild flowers and plants are, as a result, being 'standardized' to extinction.

Where has our wilderness gone? Some of it is still there but now it's in the form of public parks and preservation areas, and the footpaths which once lead through forests now lead through corn fields.

The widespread habit of making conifers rather than hardwood planta-tions for the Forestry Commission (though I must add the Commission has been most helpful in trying to conserve wild flowers in other directions) has been removing the native woodland plants and replacing them with a botanically less interesting area inside the newly created forest.

As land was cleared curved hard-wood hedgerows were grown around the perimeter and these were a haven for wildlife. The Enclosure Acts meant that hedgerows planted by the enclosing owner were generally those which would grow most quickly, as this established the owner's right to the land for all to see. These were usually of the quickthorn type, which produced a fast thick impenetrable fence layered every two years or so to make it stronger. These fences were made straight to take in the largest acreage and thus their actual length was much shorter than that of the old type barriers. Later hedgerows were seen to divide fields into too small units to be economical so many fences were removed until now there is about one fifth the length of hedgerow per acre that there used to be in the Middle Ages and of course the process still goes on. The modern idea that the hedges harbour pests over the winter and their replacement by wire railings is just the last step in the removal of one of the wild flowers' favourite habitats.

The cause of half the trouble over flower extinction is the hangover from the era when all those plants which were not crop were covered by the all embracing word weed; to be removed. Indeed we find that books on agricultural pests contained many beautiful flowers like *Georgias Manual of Weeds* for instance. In this you will find just about every plant I will ask you to grow: roses, celandines, buttercups, the lot. It is such a pity that some plants, now becoming extremely rare, are still being eradicated by farmers. The corn cockle, corn marigold, ragged robin, delightful flowers but all being ruthlessly removed and I think that in a way we all, farmers or non-farmers think of them as weeds because they are non-functional in an age of functionalism and efficiency.

A great crime is the writing off of some plant species as unworthy, for no better reason than they grow naturally. Let us take red Deadnettle as an example; 'Should be eradicated by persistent hoeing, hand pulling and with the use of root crops'; 'Moderate use of MCPA has proved effective' etc. If one looks a little closer however it comes to light that this plant 'is easily controlled by hand . . . it is propagated by seed; it is an annual and produces prolific blooms from April to October' but, of course, it is a 'weed' and so we mustn't grow it. Just looking through the weed catalogues explains why the gardener has his work cut out: digging out all the roots of brambles and removing all the speedwell before seeding; The same goes for willowherb, white Deadnettle and many other lovelies.

What about all those wild flowers you've been relentlessly pulling out all those years as weeds? Can you think of any of them that you just might get fed up with removing one of these days? Buttercups? Are there any of those plants for which ICI sell a selective weed killer, to leave your lawn totally intact (apart from a few brown holes for a while) which you could leave to grow? Daisies?

Wouldn't it be nice not to have to (gardening-book rule) fill your time with maintaining the order of your garden against the 'chaos' of beautiful wild flowers.

In 1770 John Hill a medical member of the Royal Academy said: 'The plants of our own country will cure all its diseases.' And, who am I to say that columbine will not cure jaundice. This, I think just shows the reverence with which wild flowers were treated in the past and how this has slipped away. As we come to them I will point out the supposed medicinal properties of the flowers attributed to them, at the same time pointing out the scent of the plant.

Just imagine green long grasses, rye, oats, mingled with white parsley, pink milkmaid to produce an English natural meadow, waiting for the clover and the poppies to spring a little red onto the scene. Think of the sun on that and imagine just how boring a square of allysum seems in comparison.

Let your mind wander over the wood anemonies, primroses and celandines peeping out of a hedge, almost reaching out and grabbing the insects that they were designed to attract. An oak tree with ivy and honeysuckle growing up it, gorgeous convulvulus and bindweed competing for a place on the wall, dandelions, daisies, buttercups, speedwell, thistles, standing around waiting to be admired as a sea of colour. It makes garden flowers look a bit tame but if you ask nicely or just don't spend half your time discouraging them then wild flowers will come to you and stay.

CHAPTER TWO

The Collection Tray and the Practicalities

It is not quite as easy to find seeds for the wild flowers as it sounds; few dealers stock them for the British market and some plants are not exactly superabundant in the wild. The dispersal mechanism that herbs use did not have human carriage in mind when they were designed – much rather wind, water and animals were the chosen vectors. Perhaps one day a strain will appear with a sign on it to attract *our* attention to pick and disperse fruits: 'Free garden seeds, help yourself'! We already spread a few plants through our agricultural actions (e.g. seed impurities) and our foods like the tomato with seeds that pass straight through us undigested, to appear growing in profusion at the sewage works. Until the day comes that we become a major wild flower distributor it is going to be difficult to get hold of seeds. Watch flowers as they fade and shake out the seeds as soon as they ripen, tie a muslin bag over the seeding sprays, collect the progeny in it and pick dry seed pods just in the hope that seeds are still around. With some species it is easy – like the poppy which cannot distribute the seeds into the wind fast enough and keeps a head full of them for some time. With others it is difficult however – like the violet which drops them almost as soon as they are ready, to be lost in the surrounding soil. You must decide through experience the collection process with the best results but as a general rule harvest seeds just before dispersal.

Dormancy is a process by which seeds do not germinate as soon as they are shed but rather wait on a certain time (the dormancy period) before doing so. We have relatively few plants that germinate whatever the time of year or weather because, being a temperate country, plants have to survive a fairly hard winter, which is easy as a seed but difficult as a vulnerable plant. Seeds may rest for a set period before coming up, they may be triggered by some external factor like spring warmth or sunlight, they may have tough coats, which are impermeable to water until the spring bugs have removed it, or many other factors that keep them sleeping. Anyway, my job here is to show you how to break the dormancy and allow you to set the seeds when you like.

The causes of dormancy are many; just like the ways to deal with it. Large, hard seeds (broom, gorse) cannot take in water to grow with so scrape a piece of this testa away with a file or sandpaper, soften the coat with concentrated acid, or leave the whole thing in a bag of moist soil (about twice as much soil as seeds) until the coat has rotted thin and then plant out. Some seeds need a winter – even an artificial one – warmth after which triggers sprouting, a criterion that applies to most of the plants in this book. Keep these in the cold or even almost freeze them for up to three months – a process called stratification, which should render them fit for germination. Just warmth will start up some seeds like shepherd's purse but others (some lilies) need warmth to form a seed root and then transient cold to cause a shoot to be produced.

Despite all these new-fangled techniques still one of the most effective is simply to plant the seeds at the time collected – just as in nature. Assuming it is a non-ephemeral plant then the following year will see a large percent of germinators but remember that it may leave a good few still dormant until the spring after that. This is the plant-kingdom's way of ensuring that one bad year doesn't kill off a species – because many don't come up in that year, they are safe underground.

Seed storage is not really much of a problem for land plants, they last a good long time in general when kept dry in named manilla envelopes. The mallows for instance will go for 50–100 years before losing their good germinating property and some seeds have been found buried for 1800 years that still do well. Others, however, typically those of trees, need planting out within about a week of having been shed or they will die. At the 4–5 year mark it is pretty usual for most dry seeds to become markedly infertile but this is rarely a problem because by that time you will usually have got more. Dryness preserves and the lower the water content the longer seeds last is the general rule as long as the water content of the seed does not drop below five percent (severe dessication) at which point its proteins are damaged. Dry like this they can stand temperature fluctuations of $-250°C$ to $-100°C$ or get covered by the mercury fungicides that are normally toxic and still survive. Do not worry if you find that fewer and fewer of stored seeds survive as the age of the collection increases because this is absolutely natural and, indeed, every ten years scientists are still monitoring samples of seeds buried deliberately in the nineteenth century to understand the way in which age decreases their viability.

Cultivation from seed

There are many ultra complex ways of getting seeds to grow, most of them unnecessarily tedious but just for the record I will detail here the method for one of them that I consider to produce excellent, weed-free plants.

A container, fairly deep (8cm) by modern standards is used, filled at the bottom with broken crockery, ashes, pebbles or anything extremely porous to give a good, even, drainage. This 1cm layer is covered with coarsely chopped leaves; dead oak or elm will do to prevent the soil working its way through into the drainage bed. On top of that goes a sieved compost, sterilized with fungicide if you like, giving a layer of about 2cm. From there to near the top goes sterile soil, a little sand that has been heated to a high temperature in the oven, plus chopped sphagnum moss for instance.

Calcicole (lime-loving) plants should be given a little lime in this layer, by the way, but it need not be much (the idea being to give a medium where the seed will not be attacked by fungi but will have the water that is needed for germination). Few minerals are in fact needed for the initial stages in which the radicle (little root) will get to the compost because so much nutrient is stored in the seed. Within the top layer the seeds should be put either very close to the surface if they are small (and in which case the sterile layer should only be about 2cm thick) or up to 4cm down for the larger ones.

These pans are now moistened in about 2cm of water, which will percolate up from the bottom, put in the greenhouse (early spring) or the cold frame (mid-spring) and left to grow germinating seeds. Please make sure that when planted the seeds aren't too close together because this is the quick way to get small stunted seedlings (remember the competition) and separate any tiny plants that look as if they may be strangling each other. Anyway, when they are old enough to handle remove the seedlings gently to separate stations either outside (the hardy and tenacious ones) into a nursery bed for those that can do with protection, or still under glass for those that you have forced early or do not harden easily.

Do not give too much of anything, light, heat, cold, water etc. In fact don't let the young plants or seedlings get bombarded by extremes or rapidly changing conditions. Do not take the results of germination in gentle heat in February and just plant them out directly because the frost will get them. A gentlemanly approach of giving them time to adapt, hardening off by gradually decreasing the temperature to that of the out-side, will increase their ability to survive the cold no end.

Fertilisers are all right in the embryological stage, so to speak, when the seeds are making first growth but when in the garden they should not be needed; after all, these are the plants which normally grow there without encouragement and fertilisers may (in fact will) encourage others – true weeds.

Division. Or is it multiplication?

All the way through I will be pointing out the possibility of dividing up the clump into many smaller pieces so that the stock has room to breathe and growth can increase (if that's required). It is a case where every part is fighting for scarce root and light resources and division is the means by which the parts are separated and the competition stopped. It is a suitable method for any plant that crawls rooting as it goes (restharrow or the Rock roses) gradually expands as a clump (deadnettle or mint) or sends long underground stems that resurface at intervals and flower (willowherb, bindweed).

The method is simple – just divide the plant into as many rooted, shooted parts as you can, chopping them apart with a spade if necessary, and replant them separately in a similar situation. Early spring is the best time for it, though autumn is usually pretty favourable as well.

The regenerative capacity of divided plants is often astonishing, often multiplying their size in the first year, though possibly neither flowering nor showing signs of competition fatigue.

The removal and replanting of offset bulbs or corms is in fact roughly the same process as that above because these organs are merely food store swollen leaves or stem bases. In autumn split them off with a knife if necessary from the parent plant and replant as soon as possible in a convenient, similar spot in a nursery bed to be given garden rights the following spring.

Cuttings

Softwood cuttings really bring the greatest success here and they are the ones I will stress although hardwood ones for the few woody species mentioned will be fine. Wait until there is some nice looking new growth by the plant; June should be a good time for most. If possible, make sure that the shoot in question is not wasting energy by having flowering buds and remove it from the main stem. An 8–10cm twiglet, green, still growing, is the usual recommendation but in many species there just isn't the shoot length and a much shorter affair will have to replace this. Strip this shoot from the main support or cut it just below a node, cutting off the corresponding leaf at the same time at its base (a node is a swelling of the stem where a leaf joins it) with a very sharp knife or razor blade. Dip the cut shoot base into some rooting hormone (this is not strictly necessary, mind you) and plant it vertically, an inch down in the soil you have prepared.

Soil sterilisation will help to keep the unwanted away and stop the shoot rotting but again this is not strictly necessary. Covered by a glass jar, polythene or cold frame, the cutting should be given a light, though not fully sunlit position with plenty of moisture around to seep up through the soil from below. This water supply is required to promote rooting which will be greatly delayed if it is either swamped or parched and should take from ten to thirty days.

Every now and then you give each cutting a gentle tug to see if rooting has started and once 1cm worth of root has grown it is a good idea to either (if this is July) plant out directly or (if August) to give it a place in a pot until the following year.

Layering

This is really a method akin to division because the process involves separating two rooted pieces, but it differs in that, through sheer craft, the roots of the shoot to be moved are artificially induced. Take a long shoot in summer, remove a piece of bark from the underside (about 2cm long and 5mm wide will do), dust the bared area with rooting hormone and bend it down so that this area is below soil level whereas the rest of the shoot is not. To keep it like this put a weight on top or peg it in to the soil and just wait. After a few weeks there should be a reasonable growth of new root from the scaled area so split it from the main plant just where it leaves the soil and transplant the new rooted segment. Many species do not require rooting hormone and many, especially the creeping type, will not need pegging down but each of these procedures helps to ensure the quality of the end result.

Root cuttings, leaf cuttings, bud cuttings – try them by all means – I'm sure you'll succeed. Remember, though, that all the methods apart from using seeds will produce plants exactly the same as the parent so choose your characteristics with care.

Collecting plants from the wild: A Warning

I certainly don't want anyone to think that I condone this type of action where it is applied to the removal of scarce plants that are generally a pleasure to see in their natural habitat. **It is also illegal to remove them and do remember that! Those I suggest are worth considering are only those that will do well in your garden, will replace themselves in the wild and do not cause anxiety to the landowner.** I doubt very much if old Farmer Giles will chase you off his land, threatening the law, if you ask him for some thistles – after all he will have spent a long time trying to think of ways to get rid of them. Knapweeds, colt's foot, bluebells, restharrow, fumitory – any plant that he treats as a weed will not be a problem. Around London now it is difficult to find a primrose, impossible in just country walking to find a cowslip, uncommon in many parts to see a foxglove. They have gone because some selfish person decided that he could get his plants free or a farmer decided that he could sell a valuable crop he did not plant. **Don't take plants that are dwindling, are on their own, or without permission.**

Annuals are hardly worth the bother of the process unless you'd like them to self seed in your garden whereas perennials certainly are, they are going to give plenty of scope for propagation and will live a long time.

Throughout the book I've stressed the exact processes of horticulture and to be a little hard on myself it is not usually as difficult as the precise methods make out. Transplantation within the garden for instance can take place with most plants throughout the year, it is just that some need very expert gardeners to be able to carry it off. The same is true of transplantation from the wild. The more soil taken, the greater the success – that's my motto. When I say to move them in spring or autumn for instance, then these are the times when the least soil will be needed and the greatest ease encountered. Dig deep enough around the roots, maybe bringing one cubic foot away with a 60cm tall plant, and wrap this immediately in newspaper or polythene to prevent water and soil loss. Don't allow the tall ones to fall over – a usual trick of things like meadowsweet because they may injure the stem and prevent the roots getting the nourishment necessary for 'taking' as well as losing the flower. The longer it is left like this, wrapped up, the more chance there is of dehydration, damage or death so get it back to the old homestead and into its final home right smartish, watering it as necessary on the way. The surface creeper types like the speedwell are ones that, like stonecrops, need not be given a great deal of soil to pacify them but most plants will demand a good clod so do not go out expecting to forage 20 plants because unless your car goes in for weight lifting, or your army does, it is going to be impractical. Flowers will grow best in similar spots to their natural home. Don't put humusy woodland plants in a lime garden and expect the soil of transplantation will keep them going because this may be fine for the first year but very quickly those hydrogen ions that kept the soil acid will have leached out and left your hard-earned plant with soil it does not like. Just try this on wood anemonies or primroses and watch them die and then perhaps you'll feel like sticking to your own soil's native plants.

Weeds and controlled growth

It certainly must never be denied that you are going to have trouble with turncoat rampant plants. Doubtless no one can tell you exactly the habitat requirement to keep the most aggressive species under control so this section is included to make sure that ordinary methods can be used in an emergency (like a gardenful of nightshade). But please look again at your so-called weeds. This book aims to make you think twice before massacring what can often be beautiful plants if handled intelligently.

There are about 250 million poppy seeds per hectare of arable land (that's 25,000 per square metre) all layered down years earlier. Billions of other seeds wait in the soil for the right conditions to make themselves felt. The poppies of Flanders came up around the graves in the 1914–18 war because they had been buried by nature years earlier and the ground disturbance gave them their chance.

First line of action towards stopping their spread is mechanical; remove seed pods before they are ripe, plant slates around the spreaders (vertically to form a wall above and below the surface), weed out all the unfavourable plants, flame away weeds, bury pernicious ones like buttercups and nettles by digging, persistently cut them with a hoe or lawnmower or plant large strong favourable spreaders around them. I'd like to say that there would be marvellous methods of biological control by natural pests for the common weeds but the problem is that they are mostly recent introductions to Britain that have come without their natural enemies so they grow unabated.

The prickly pear cactus spread like wild-fire when first introduced into Australia as a fodder crop, but the following of the insect that laid its eggs inside has decimated its Aussie population. Perhaps there are potent insect antagonists of willowherb or sticky groundsel somewhere but right now you may have to rely on herbicides to deal with them and other weeds.

Nothing in the herbicidal range is a good substitute for good management of a garden. We do very extensive damage to our soil by the use of poisons like herbicides and pesticides but they need to be included here because, despite ecological methods, certain plants are bound to get out of control though not as badly as you might at first think.

Difficulty in herbicide usage arises in wet weather with the low concentration hormone types, windy weather with dusts or sprays (drastic results down wind especially with hormones and DNOC, which has a poisonous vapour) and close to wanted plants, especially in the rock garden or the summer bed. They can be divided up artificially into the selective and non-selective types but really it is just the degree of selectivity that changes because they all affect some plants more than others. Here is a gardeners assortment of them in probably the order of selectivity with the most generally lethal first.

Sodium chlorate, the famed destroyer of all, is not as inflammable as was once made out because commercial preparations contain flame controllers but it is pretty effective on almost any plant. It keeps away all comers for about three months, with the six month mark the time to re-introduce flowers. Use 4–16 oz per 10 square metres either scattering or dissolving in $\frac{1}{2}$–2 gallons of water and pouring it on (careful not to go within 15cm of the border).

Arsenical compounds – avoid these for the children's sake.

Cyanamides – act as a fertiliser too, used in cereal crops.

Lawn sand and contents; a mixture in the ratio of 4 : 1 : 1 of sand, ammonium sulphate and iron sulphate, which, lightly sprinkled on the lawn, will remove the broader leaved plants like daisies, dandelions and plantains. It also has a fertiliser action.

DNOC and the coal-tar derivatives now have many plants immune to them but nettles still succumb. There are better ones around.

Hormone growth promoters used at a concentration of about one part per thousand kill most effectively dicotyledons, though irregularly even against them. At low concentrations growth is markedly accelerated by them because they are derivatives of hormone chemicals by which the plant regulates its growth. The effect is similar to that of the defoliants used in Vietnam, which are in fact leaf inducers at low doses but leaf removers at high doses. The cunning chemists came up with a substance 2.4 DB, which is converted in some plants but not others into the hormone 2.4-D by the plant's own cells. This substance in turn acts as a herbicide and kills the plant. If you use any of the proprietary forms of these chemicals choose a fine day to apply it and wash out the watering can afterwards because even taints of the stuff do considerable damage.

Hardly a month goes by now without someone somewhere improving or smartening processes to deal with weeds. Stacks of preparations are used now including the famous paraquat, which either enters plants through leaf and stem or is broken down quickly in the soil so its effect there is not too great and fresh plants can be put in as soon as the weeds have died.

Below is the list of persistent offenders that warrant individual treatment as to their herbicidal tendencies. They all have invasive and pernicious roots which need a slowly acting weed killer because this indicates that some of the poison is getting down that far.

Bindweed—Lesser. This has such amazingly efficient spreading properties that if it were green and ordinary, I would never consider it for the garden. Roots going 10 metres down from the stem, up to 3 metres down from the surface, an overkill of seeds well scattered every year, it's a long-lasting as well as a pretty but invasive plant. MCPA or one of the expensive modern chemicals will discourage it extensively but don't you find it a shame to do away with it?

Bindweed—Greater. Large, fine plants that are beautiful and would perhaps take over the world, if they went on with the increase we have seen in them over the last few years here. It has large roots, should succumb to many herbicides but its seeds last for ages in the soil.

Colt's foot. Tedious weeding, mowing down regularly of the leaves, pulling off the fertilized flowers (they bend over once pollinated), planting slates around the patch, and non-selective weed killers will keep it in check. Often it grows in pretty impoverished parts of the garden only, so its almost worth keeping.

Daisies. Don't you like daisies? Lawn sand will get rid of them if you're that way inclined but they're rarely an aesthetic problem.

Dandelions. The two common dry soil types at least, get the chop from either lawn sand particularly in the autumn or 2.4-D. The dandelion doesn't have a sexual reproductive cycle – the flower is only there for the show but it produces seeds (not so many as the hawkweeds) in quite large numbers. The long tap root is in a state of contraction, almost dragging the rosette of leaves down into the soil, so you will find it difficult to grub up the plant by its roots.

Hawkweeds of various kinds seem to succumb fairly well either to lawn sand or to broadcast ammonium sulphate.

Knapweeds. MCPA is a reasonable show stopper here but prevention of seeding is the real necessary measure to prevent being overrun by them.

Ragworts. Pull them up, if you must! (the seeds will ripen anyway if the plant is just left out so put it on the compost heap and cover it), dust them with ammonium sulphate, give 2.4-D during flowering, or bring in the cinabar moth or ragwort seedfly and eventually it will go. Agriculturally it needs cutting down to ground level twice in the same year to kill it so if all else fails perhaps that simple method will be some help.

Sow Thistle. Repeated doses of 2.4-D or MCPA will eventually get the huge root systems going. Thistles in general are often only semi-fertile, spreading generally by vegetative means like suckers. Get them at the pre-flowering stage with DCPA or MCPA and just hope – because there are resistant types around. Chlorate will do the job if it fails.

White Deadnettle. I was going to say that I had bad news because there isn't really much that will get them down, but the truth is that they can be beaten by sodium chlorate or some of the newer brands.

Willowherb. Much like many perennials may be cut down regularly to produce a clean result after a year or so.

Yarrow. Sodium chlorate works fine when scattered on a clump and it will just have to do because selectives are pretty ineffective.

Diseases

Well, I could go on and on all day because, quite naturally, there are nasties here for just about every species, whereas imported garden flowers tend either not to be much affected or to succumb totally. The gall midge of St John's wort, the root diseases of wood anemonies, and the susceptibility of imported rose roots to our soil bugs; the subject is enormous. If you get epidemics then remove and burn affected plants, but don't worry, the garden will always recover in time – inevitably, because if the plant is killed by a disease then that agent dies as well and it would never exist for long. Our wild flowers are resistant to many of the horrors that ravage imported ones. We're lucky, so make use of it. *Support your local agriculture!*

Some weeds harbour pests of agricultural crops through different parts of their life cycle; agrimony harbours hop mildew, tansy gives a home to sunflower rust and so on.

Here are the major plants that you're liable to want but which the farmer of the field next door may object to: agrimony, colt's foot, cranesbills, meadowsweet, corn mint, restharrow, scabious, shepherd's purse, thistles in general, tansy, willowherb and yarrow. Of course there are many more disease-harbouring plants, more and more appearing with research, but these are the main ones and shouldn't be grown in too vast a quantity without telling the farmer next door.

First steps

You have decided to embrace the wilderness and need to know where to start. Of course there is no need to pull up your conventional cultivated plants wholesale. Wild plants and flowers can be infiltrated into spare niches as and when the opportunity arises. For the present purpose, though, I have given here plans of whole gardens given over to wild flowers. They are meant to stimulate and guide, but *you* are the arbiter of your own garden design.

The first step is to take stock of your own patch and draw up a sketch plan (like plan A) of its ecological make-up. All gardens differ, of course, but there are common elements found in each one: shade, moisture, acidity, etc. Here in our 'average' garden they are marked in together with those features which are permanent like trees, walls, paths or lawns. Also mark in direction of sun, wind exposure, general orientation – in fact anything which is likely to affect the plants you want to grow. In addition, there are inexpensive and uncomplicated gadgets available at most garden centres and shops which will indicate the degree of acidity in your soil (pH). The average pH is 7.

Having taken stock of the habitat you must now choose the wild plant to fit. Chapter 4 gives plants in order of garden usefulness and catalogues them by basic characteristic: climbing, creeping, ground cover, water plants, etc. In addition Appendix 1 gives a cross reference guide to plants that, for example, love chalk, hate lime, are early or late flowering, are tall or short and so on. Thus you will be able to fit a wild plant into a space in the garden to which it is suited and get it to do the job you want it to do.

Plan B gives an example of a garden completely given over to wild plants. Here they are being used fairly conventionally, more or less duplicating the function of cultivated plants. Do not be hide-bound, though, by traditional ideas of 'neatness'. Go for massed plants which give a feeling of lush wildness and, incidentally, help each other along. The design suggested here is quite

Plan A

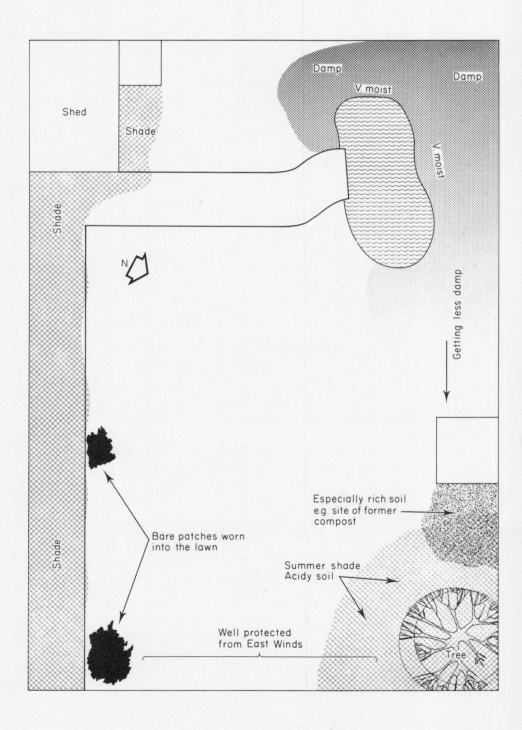

loose and suits the plants' characteristics.

Plan B shows a garden which is damper towards the west; so, starting anti-clockwise (1) one sees a bare patch of lawn (where the children always make their entry). It needs a strong and sturdy plant to deter them. *Comfrey* is an especially good choice because it is slightly rough, tall, with large leaves and sprays of beautiful blue flowers. It does, however, tend to overgrow so it might be a good idea to put it next to a restraining wall. At the back of the north-easterly bed I have put *St John's Wort* which does not need a large soil supply but will make good use of the light, thus growing to match its comfrey neighbour. The primroses will act as a restraining 'wall' for the taller St John's Wort. Plant them close together and with the violets they will all benefit from a slightly acid soil condition.

The northern corner is separated from the bed we have just discussed by a mowable daisy-and-dandelion strip which acts as a sort of 'fire-break' between the rather conventionally laid-out bed and the wilder patch of this north corner. Nettles and thistles will attract all sorts of butterflies and bees and the *Dog's Mercury* next to them thrives on low light levels and will compete with and contain the nettles. *Herb Robert* is a low leafy herb with lovely pink flowers – a perfect border plant which does not spread too much and thrives in half shade.

There is little need, I hope, to explain the choice of *Bluebells*. Shade loving they are the perfect complement to Dog's Mercury. It is early-flowering and prolific. Still in the shade but now moving up the north-western wall we find *Celandines* with their low yellow star-shaped flowers and *Wood Anemones*. Because they like the same type of habitat as bluebells they will act as a containing wall. *Cowslips* guard the border (towards the end of the season they might need to be reinforced with *Campion* to keep out interlopers.

Common Mallow was chosen for the western side of the cold frame because it prefers (though does not insist on) damper ground with good sun. It will form a slowly spreading and bushy plant with beautiful pink flowers. It will keep to itself but will limit the *Meadowsweet* and *Deadnettle* next to it. The meadowsweet likes the damper ground and with its tall white flowers is perfect as a background. The *White Deadnettle* or *Archangel* (a yellow flowered relative) both have extensive greenery which may, towards the end of the year, encroach on the *Stitchwort*. However, deadnettle is more attractive than its stinging cousin so the invasion may not be entirely unwelcome. The stitchwort will act as a spring border plant and likes damp ground.

Now into the really damp part of the garden by the pond. Autumn *crocuses* should do well in the grass which protects them from choking weeds. Around the pool are four plants. *Forget-me-not* was chosen for its charming sprays of flowers appearing through its plentiful foliage. Water mint is not so much a culinary herb as a tall green plant with purple flowers. The *Yellow flag* is very sturdy, as is *Policeman's Helmet* and these will help contain the mint. *Monkey Flower* and *Kingcups* like the same very damp not too acid

Plan B

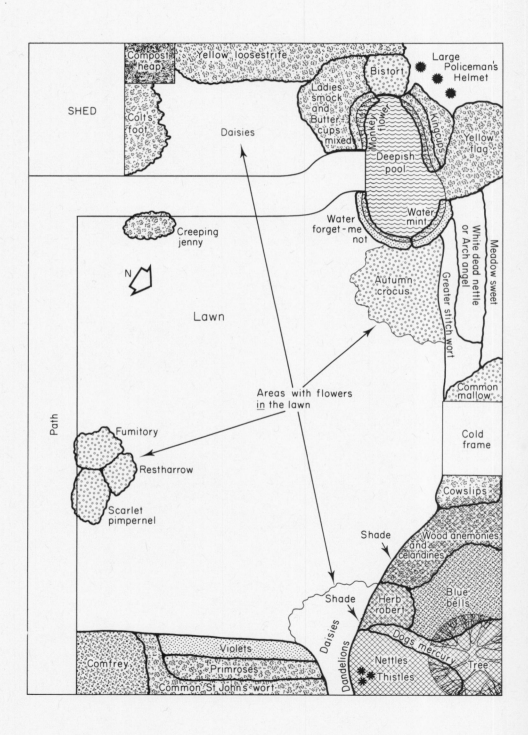

soil and will thus, through competition for the same ecological niche, control each other. The *Bistort* between them could act as a 'referee'. Yellow Flag is a tough spectacular iris with strong pointed leaves growing from a close mass at its base. The Bistort is a rush-like plant with thin pointed leaves and long flowering stalk growing from a dense root base. It will stand out splendidly against the shorter plants at its sides. Policeman's Helmet, with its large leaves, strong roots and love of the damp should swamp this corner with high pink flowers.

On the western side we find a patch of lawn next to the path. At the back *Yellow Loosestrife* will make a pretty three-foot high backdrop and will vigorously resist the incursions of buttercup or *Ladies' Smock*. The *Colt's Foot* needs a sunny spot and, being tallish will stand out well against the shed.

Now for the lawn. The *Creeping Jenny* loves damper spots which are not too overpowered by taller plants. Let it spread onto the path, edging it with yellow/green. As with most lawns we have the problem of bare patches. Here, *Fumitory*, *Restharrow* and *Scarlet Pimpernel*, all of which like dry spots and plenty of sun away from taller plants. They will quickly green the bare patches and, each will give a red flower of different hue later in the summer.

If you mow the lawn this, together with the path and natural competition will control the plants' spread and where once was brown earth you will see a vibrant red patch. The garden just described does not exist (yet) but it does contain a number of the features and problems which can be experienced in many gardens.

Plan C represents a much more homogenous habitat with an average pH of 6.5. It is the average London or Home Counties garden type. The plants here have been arranged in accordance with their compatibility (or lack of it if you want them to control each other) and suitability for the prevailing conditions. It has been designed to give you good colour display, height control and ease of maintainance.

Plan D is of a garden dominated by dryness, good sunshine, neutral soil and featuring a rockery. Again I have gone for banked clumps which will create a sense of profusion and, of course, resist the invasion of unwanted plants.

Plan C

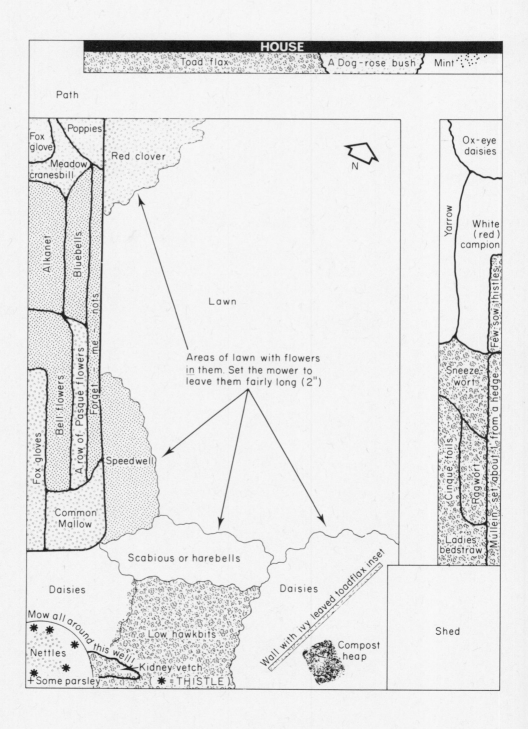

HOUSE

Toad flax   A Dog-rose bush   Mint

Path

Fox glove

Poppies

Meadow cranesbill

Red clover

N

Alkanet

Bluebells

Forget - me - nots.

Lawn

Areas of lawn with flowers in them. Set the mower to leave them fairly long (2")

Fox gloves

Bell flowers

A row of, Pasque flowers

Speedwell

Common Mallow

Scabious or harebells

Daisies

Daisies

Mow all around this well!

❋ ❋

Nettles

❋

a. Low hawkbits

❋

+ Some parsley

Kidney vetch

(❋ = THISTLE)

Wall with ivy leaved toadflax inset

Compost heap

Shed

Ox-eye daisies

Yarrow

White (red) campion

Few sow thistles

Sneeze wort

Cinque foils

Ragwort

Mullein: set about from a hedge

Ladies bedstraw

Plan D

31

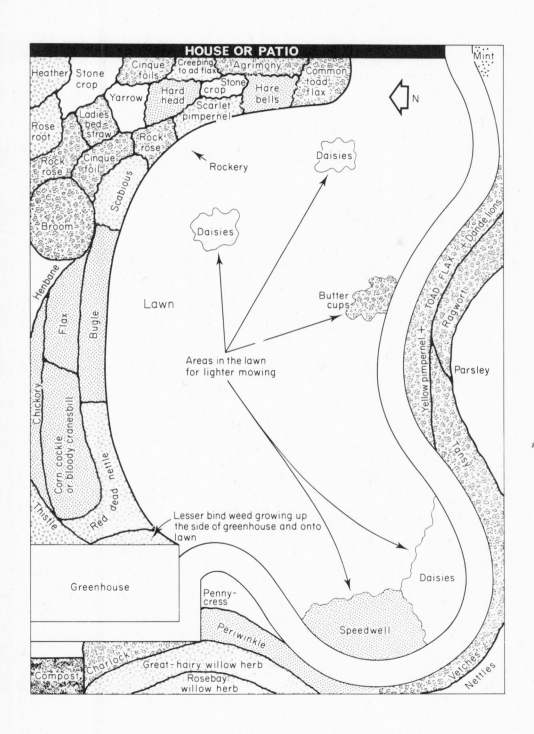

HOUSE OR PATIO

Heather | Stone crop | Cinque foils | Creeping to ad flax | Agrimony | Common toad flax

Mint

Yarrow | Hard head | Stone crop | Hare bells

Ladies bed straw | Scarlet pimpernel

Rose root | Rock rose | Cinque foil | Rock rose

N

Broom

Scabious

Rockery

Daisies

Daisies

Henbane

Flax

Bugle

Lawn

Butter cups

Yellow pimpernel + TOAD FLAX + Dande lions

Ragwort

Parsley

Chickory

Corn cockle or bloody cranesbill

Red dead nettle

Areas in the lawn for lighter mowing

Tansy

Thistle

Lesser bind weed growing up the side of greenhouse and onto lawn

Greenhouse

Penny-cress

Daisies

Periwinkle

Speedwell

Compost

Charlock

Great-hairy willow herb

Rosebay willow herb

Vetches

Nettles

CHAPTER THREE

Ecological Gardening

If you leave all the windows of your house open, you needn't be surprised if you get burgled, and similarly if you leave great holes in your garden policy don't be shocked by invading plants stealing the spaces you've left. By this I mean that something however small and insignificant will take up the smallest, leanest offer of a living if it is left over by your garden management: Making sure that the ecological niches that would be filled by enemy plants normally are filled by friendly ones is the whole idea of this book and the procedure is to be economical, to use up all the available resources you have.

Ecology derives its name from the Greek 'oikos', which means house or dwelling and oikos has given rise to the word economy as this waste-not attitude has dominated the living world for millions of years until now every available spot capable of supporting life is colonized. The gardener, to suit himself, is always trying to push the environment further and further away from the natural, stable, regimen and thus he must guard every door or the wilds will return to drag the garden back to ecological equilibrium. Wild is stable. Garden is artificial and normally unstable.

The traditional horticulturalist plucks out dutifully all the things that offend him and back they grow after a short spell. He is undeterred. As a child my father used to drag me into the garden every week to weed the beds and hoe and tend. 'He must be crazy,' I thought. All over the jungle (relatively speaking) that inhabited the back garden were plants struggling amongst each other for breathing space, using every weapon in their armoury to make it seed at the expense of everything else. And yet, here we were, cleaning and polishing one small patch only feet away from the writhing morass of willowherb and nettles, which were of course aching to get at the 'New World' where they could grow unobstructed. Any seeds or shoots that made it to the bare spot must have thought it was their lucky day.

That piece of bare ground which we cleared of nettles, must have been in some way special to nettles; they grew there at the expense of some other creeping plant originally so when the position became vacant again they are just as favoured as they were at the start and will probably grow back (there's a large element of chance as well). Like the proverbial mouse on the treadmill, the gardener is working hard to stand still. He knows they will grow back. Admittedly the attitude of 'clear the whole garden of weeds and you won't have any problem' is all very fine if you don't mind spending ages and empires doing it and protecting the place from the seeds from next door. There is a better way.

It seems obvious that replacement therapy for this scrap of ground is what is needed; getting something else to grow in the spot and keep down the nettles or, at least, slow them down a bit. At this job, incidently plants are better than concrete as everyone knows nettles will just grow around mechanical obstructions with extra vigour.

The ability of any particular species to get its seeds to grow in the newly available soil is like the ability of one advertiser to get his message across better than a competitor. He that gets to the client first, takes hold of the market fastest, bombards the buyers with the greatest quantity and has a modicum of luck gets the contract. So giving the chosen plants that competitive edge over the weedy rivals means giving them a head start by planting seedlings of a slow grower like campion and letting this time advantage allow it to choke out the unwanteds. Then again it could mean killing a fly with a shotgun and planting far more of the desired plant than the weeds can resist, e.g. sprinkling liberally with poppy seeds, knowing that enough of them will stop weed development. Taking hold of the plot faster than weeds needs a perennial or probably an annual that can overtake the rest and keep them down by its own virulence, e.g. speedwell, whose name speaks for itself. So when the nettles become a problem, the allies can be victorious simply by growing something else in their place.

The last few pages have shown how controlling and filling the niche, backing the winning horse in the plant race if you like, guards against the undesirables. But what if you don't even have a runner, a candidate for the space? Well, I'd like to show how usefully the niches can fill themselves and this is particularly true with insects as, short of spending all day with a butterfly net and a can of flyspray, controlling the fauna is a difficult task. An example: a gardener who decides to keep cabbages and weed out all the other plants around them (so they'll look pretty I suppose) finds he has a problem with the famous and ubiquitous Cabbage White butterfly, with clinical symptoms of holey leaves from the effects of the caterpillar. Now, using the first method would involve replacing the insect with another one that kept the same place in bug society but would eat the leaves less avidly, i.e. replacement therapy. Using this second way however, involves leaving the weeds that the owner spent so long removing so that the natural insect population returns and the ichneumons and braconids that feast on aphids and caterpillars do away, to an enormous extent, with the Cabbage White. Lo! the cabbages grow well and little has to be done for them. Or then again he could spray his cabbage every week in season and load the soil with insecticides.

That example was to show that nature is not only pushy to the point of taking all the spare places in the environment and filling them with life but also creates more niches by doing so. Insects grow to feed on corn, say, and then more organisms grow to feed on them. It is up to the gardener to make sure that the natural regulation that is built into the system works to help him and so not destroy the predators of enemies. The man with the spray gun who goes blindly into his vegetable patch and destroys all the weeds and insects for a short time cannot be aware of the way that nature works for him. Ecosystems are homeostatic (resist change) and will make sure that plants do not die off before seeding.

To restate the two points: to regulate the population of the plants in the garden and to maintain their viability you can:

1 Fill vacant niches with suitable, useful occupants.

2 Allow nature to fill spaces that you provide with her own candidates.

As the chances for this crafty manipulation crop up with each individual plant I will point them out.

The gardening habit has always been a slow leisurely affair with plenty of time for thought and reflection. Let us proceed at walking pace.

There are portraits by modern artists of the country farmer as a part of the land, merging into the background as a piece of nature and growing out of the earth to which he will return. This is rather truer of the nineteenth-century peasant who knew the twists and turns of the natural processes and whose children saw and felt them expand around them as they grew up. They felt, and were subservient to natures will – a feeling clearly represented in *Lark Rise to Candleford* written by Flora Thompson who had spent her childhood in such surroundings. Tremendous stability and a feeling of timelessness pervades this book and we can contrast it with the way we, as children and adults, are often totally ignorant of nature's ways now that the wilds are subservient to man's will.

The land of the last century was farmed extensively to meet the needs of an expanding population but stability was the key word, for we had to trust to nature's reserves to keep it that way.

Now our forces in horticulture are so strong and our needs so great, that the balance and stability has been taken into our hands, giving us power to do things that multiply our agricultural outputs, and also firmly placing in our hands the future of the land. When man fights nature he must think not only of the present but also of the future; he must consider the results of his actions on the generations to come. I believe that we must hand back some of this power to nature for it is only by the use of ecological methods in farming and gardening that we can hope to hold on to stability. Our under-standing of natural processes is growing and we must allow ecological stability to take a hold in agriculture and gardening.

Within an ecological system that has not reached the equilibrium of climax (where the forces for change all oppose each other) there is a slow evolution to a new system where the once predominant force is less effective – it moves towards stability. Make a piece of land bare and it is bound, within a few months, if it is in a good situation, to be covered with herbs – they are the first invaders. When a scrap of earth is left brown in the garden then sure 'as eggs are eggs' something will migrate to it. In general the newcomer will be ordinary, green and boring and the gardener will nip it out without more ado. So let me ask you if you have ever thought what the result would be if you simply left it there? Just a mass of weeds you may say. Well, yes but not just green ones. It is true that the initial invaders are not particularly attractive for they have to conserve all their energy for growing rather than flowering but often they will be superseded by larger, flowery species. That change takes time, months perhaps and it is a movement towards a more stable vegetation; flowers and larger herbs will supersede weeds if given the chance. Eventually, if left long enough I would expect the abandoned garden to return to the thriving wild and on to deciduous woodland though that last transformation would take hundreds of years and it is possible to consider an ecological garden of wild flowers as stable. As a result of this weeds should not get much of a look in and if they do you will have to look elsewhere in this book for the principles of plant population control. There you have examples of procedures but as far as the actual decisions for the garden are concerned, science is years away from concrete answers to guide you. The principles behind the changes of flora and fauna have been worked out and well documented but nevertheless the application of our knowledge to the agricultural or horticultural scene is very rudimentary. Years to come will see an improvement in this respect – so with luck the inadequacies present in any policy will be filled by future research. At the moment to be scientific 'observe nature' and copy the desired effect because flowers growing well in the natural situation should do similarly well when given a similar site in the garden. Use nature to fight the battles for the soil, let her dictate the popula-tion that you grow and let her provide you with the stability.

When walking in the country look at the flowers that grow there and observe their conditions. The thistle will be seen in pasture land as one of the few plants left standing by sheep because they don't like prickles (donkeys will eat it but they are not as partial to it as is made out in the fairy stories). Around it will be low, well cropped grass, little shade-producing foliage and probably many more, younger thistles. The next field may see it stand-ing head and shoulders above the long grass that is being grown for hay but it isn't doing so well. Quite likely that thistle was just there before the grass was allowed to grow long or was planted and was fostered in previous years by the grazing of its competitors. Bring the messages of this country walk back to the garden and give the thistle a place in an odd piece of lawn edging or where the grass has been left long for the butterflies.

Foxgloves are common flowers, very beautiful in the wild and often seen on country strolls. Maybe next time you see one it will be apparent that it likes a slightly sheltered spot in woodland margins or as part of the hedge-row. They prefer a place where water is freely available, drainage good and usually where there is not all that much immediately around to crowd them out. Bring this information back to the homestead garden policy, where it will be fruitful.

All around there are acres and acres of farmlands, swarming with plant life that can be learned from and copied. Go outside the garden to some piece of wasteland for a glimpse of what might be growing in your garden without you there to protect it. If you live in town then there is a good possibility that the local youngsters will have done away with any pretty flowers and therefore your choice of flower may be luck or the odd willowherb or any weed that you do find may prove suitable. In the country a talk to a local naturalist or a few days observation will reveal an enormous variety that grows locally.

At one time I used to live in Surrey near to Gatwick airport and around us the copses were chock ablock with wild flowers – wood anemonies, celandines, dog's mercury, bluebells, primroses etc. These used to grow well, so one day, when a little closer scrutiny of a grass verge revealed an agrimony flowerhead growing strongly this suggested that, purely because it grew nearby, it would automatically be an easy garden flower. The lessons of the surroundings cannot be appreciated well enough and the choice of flowers for the garden is one area where they are largely disregarded – just wasting valuable advice. If you want nature's inbuilt stability then apeing her schemes is just about the only way that will attract it: so learn from the lessons of the countryside and build a better garden.

Earlier the principles of ecology were given an airing and it is exactly those which govern a plant's ability or lack of it to take to your cultivation. So, before you start, decide what kind of soil, climate, temperature range, height above sea level etc. you have got and rule out all those plants that cannot put up with them.

Take the soil in the garden for instance. The alkaline soils over South-East England have a particular set of calcicole flowers which will only live on chalky ground; like thyme or some orchids. Also present will be those flowers found elsewhere that will tolerate the chalk; like mullein or mellilot. If you have calcareous soil then your choice of flowers is limited to those in the two groups above because the remainder will not abide anything non-acid (don't worry by the way, this still leaves the majority of plants for you). It is, of course, difficult to find out exactly which plants will grow in exactly which soils but normally each species has quite a wide range to go at so normally you should be able to grow most plants. The crunch comes when you discover that when in anything but one kind of soil, a plant will grow all right but will not be able to compete with other plants more suited. The best example here is of course heather, which will grow perfectly well in ordinary garden soil, but it is quickly overrun by other plants more suited to the rich (relative to the heather's normal poor diet) land. The same type of treatment goes for each of the other parameters of the environment, which can make planning a tricky business. Remember, though, that it is useless trying to grow comfrey in dry ground, primroses in alkaline soil, daisies without plenty of sun, violets without spring warmth or foxgloves in the wind – all of them are not in the spot that nature picked for them so they will falter and die.

Anyway, choose what kind of soil you've got and rule out all those plants that can't stand it – wood sorrel for instance needs soils too acid for most gardens. Then, go over the other factors and reject the flowers that do not fit from the list that remains until you are left with a short list of names of species from which to choose your new garden members. The list of plants (see pp. 122–4) will help you.

The jigsaw puzzle of how plants should be integrated starts next with deciding the way in which you will get the best view of your garden blooms with, at the same time the greatest degree of equilibrium within the plant society that is produced. To this end I have put the wild flowers and plants in categories in the next chapter as to which situation – border, ground-cover etc. to put them in. These classifications are broad, so it is up to you to decide where to put them, but bear in mind a few points as you do decide; we have very little information about how plants put together will interact so you will be learning something new but it is often possible to guess how plants will get along just by taking note of a few of their characteristics. Do not put climbers next to plants that are easily smothered – *Convulvulus arvensis* near mullein for instance. Do not put sun lovers, however tall, right back behind everything else just because they are too big – policeman's helmet likes light and should be given a free space; plant the water-lovers in the dampest places and give them good regular watering – Britain used to be a very damp place and plants like bistort still remember it. Put flowers that normally coexist together like the orchids and campions, dog's mercury (an interesting green affair) and bluebells, or buttercups and milkmaid. Plant everything closer together than would be the gardening manual standard distance, they will compete underground for nutrients and keep away weeds – foxgloves like plenty of space but 20cm is all that is needed and will ensure, usually, clear space between them. Give ground cover plants an 'edge' past which they get stopped by the other plants – for example, thyme can be surrounded by toadflax. Separate and throw away most of the clumps that are growing too fast, give them stronger, larger neighbours, until you discover a plant that will keep them under control – vetches will keep down bindweeds, which should be cut down before the vetches are planted over the top. Try not to give to them soil any better than the flowers encounter in the wild because if you do, they will leave nutrients over that weeds will come in and use.

Never give too much fertiliser – you'll be fertilising weeds more than flowers if you do. Grow long-rooted plants like charlock or bindweed over poor patches of soil because they will tend to bring up from the lower levels the minerals that can restore productivity to the ground. Plant leguminous plants like vetches or peas over patches that are short in nitrates or in poor soils where nothing else will grow because they have nitrate synthesizing roots and can make up for the deficiency. Do not let quickly spreading plants seed too freely by removing seed pods – taking away the explosive broom capsules is a laborious and not all that necessary process, whereas removal of poppy heads is certainly useful (just think of the few seeds of broom compared to the thousands of poppy). Experience of nature's ways is the best adviser of the actions to take in ecologically based cultivation. Take notice of what I say above, and use it by all means, but learn as you are gardening through unlimited consultation with the plants themselves. When, in the future you find that even the hedge is not free from invasion perhaps experience will ring the little bell that says that a niche is empty and other plants are trying to fill it. That little bell should tell you to add new species yourself to the hedge – clematis, hops, convulvulus, ivy, trees – so that the niche is filled. Just in passing a mixed hedge is an absolute blessing when it comes to ornithology because the greater the variety of scaffolding the more birds will decide to nest there.

*   *   *

The last section has dealt with the flowers, but how about the pests? Weeds I hope should not be that much of a problem (as they are in the average garden) because of the way that our national flowers are included in the beds and can defeat them at their own rabid game. British flowers should self sow fairly freely and may even become the weeds themselves, instead of the rather boring types that now plague the gardens. Weeds aren't all that bad really though; they protect bare soil against the leaching and corrosive elements, they bring useful nutrients up from the lower layers of the soil to the surface (nettles are particularly good at this, but then again so are golden rod, mullein and thistles), and they are part of the series of soil builders that keeps the ground full of organic material by donating their remains. Due to all these effects and to their ability to provide anchorage to loose soil, it is always better to have weeds on uncovered soil than to have nothing there at all.

As an aside here, let me tell you about the ways in which the modern herbicides have been changing the weeds that agriculture has to put up with.

They tend to remove those weeds that are high in density, like charlock used to be before they got around to selectively killing it, but it seems that those that are low in density to begin with, may actually be able to increase slightly in numbers because the competition is less intense. Annuals (non-weed killer resistant) are going downhill, whereas the perennials seem to be unchanged or, like the resistant annuals like chickweed, to have climbed a little. This is really encouraging news, because, although the actual number of weeds has decreased enormously (to the farmer's pleasure) the actual number of species present – including many pretty ones – has perhaps increased.

How about insects? Chemical warfare against them, which has been going on for a long time in various forms, turns out to be a poor deal with the benefits few and short-lived; long term if used at particular times (when larvae are emerging for instance), and often turning sour. Resistance to the killer chemicals builds up quickly among the fast-reproducing pests but not so fast among their slower procreating predators so all over the world there are examples of how application of pesticides has actually fostered the pests. Two examples are the Californian citrus red scale and the cyclamen mite on strawberries. The effect of the sprays is not permanent, and once removed there is often a 'rebound phenomenon' in which the pests rocket in population unabated while their predators try to eat their way to catching up. Pesticides cause other environmental damage apart from just killing the pests; they build up in the soil, in birds, in plants and go on killing, but this time it is birds or animals instead of insects that succumb. An agriculturalist tells me that 50 per cent of the pesticides used in agriculture are unnecessary – just a tribute to the good salesmanship of the chemical companies – but do not let us decry them too much because without the likes of ICI, our food productivity would be much lower. Biological pest control is the successor to the non-specific and danger-ridden chemicals but is still largely in the research stage; eventually these methods will take over if only because of economics and the problems arising through tolerance to the pest killers. We shall see methods like importation of insect predators for release, the use of insect mating attractants (pheromones) to confuse the males, chemical use to increase predator and decrease pest (a form of which has already begun), plants resistant to pests, replacement in the ecological system of pests by non-pests, or perhaps the use of sterilized male insects to produce unfertile pest eggs but the garden application of these are far off and the chemicals used now are the major controlling factor. Remember the damage that they do to the soil, the birds and the animals, remember that most wild flowers can look after themselves, thank you, and use much less in future – there is little place for them in the wild garden, and I ask you to consider ecological methods of control first of all – and last too.

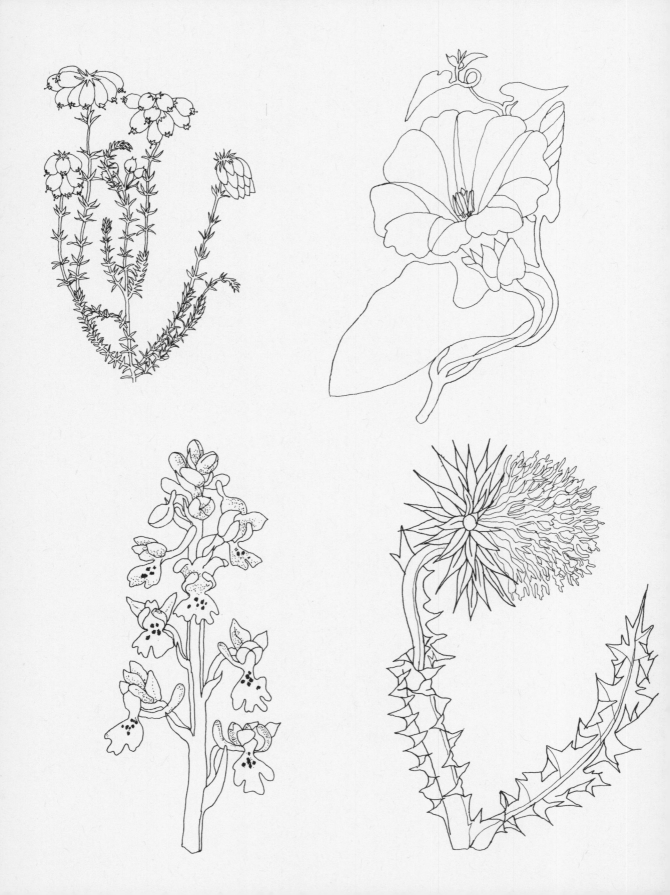

Flowers in Abundance :
A Grower's Directory of Plants

The candidates that I have included here are those which most people will
be able to cultivate; there are many more, indeed legions of rarer flowers
that make vastly more attractive effects in the wild, but not quite so much
is known about them. Certainly try them in your garden but remember
rarer flowers become rarer from mishandling. Perhaps it might be best to
try your hand at some of the flowers I have detailed first but remember
there will need to be some variation of application throughout the country.

The plants are divided up into artificial categories but please do not just
rule out a plant because it is in the wrong section for your needs; rock
roses are pretty happy outside the rockery for instance. Simply consider all
the information given and decide for yourself whether a plant that you
like may fill a space – you soon know if you are right.

All are easy to cultivate so the order in which you find them in the book –
each section in decreasing order of garden usefulness (i.e. the best towards
the beginning) should tell you something about their weedy invasive
properties as well as their beauty. So without further ado, may I introduce
these high hopes of herbaceous harmony, these flowers of flirtation's
fortune – the plants themselves.

Herbaceous plants
for the border and bed

Foxglove. *Digitalis purpurea.*
   Biennial. Ordinary soil, sandy especially.
Well, this must be one of the great triumphs of the 'let's grow wild flowers' people like myself because in the early nineteenth century, following an attack on the neglect of British wild flowers by a prominent horticultural-ist, it was originally grown as a garden plant in this country. Can you imagine that this plant was left alone, itself one of the most beautiful of flowers, while the world was scoured, with great effort on the behalf of the botanists, just to find pretty foreign ones? Throughout this chapter I shall describe the medical uses to which each plant has been put and, I suppose derive a little pleasure as a medically trained person to think that we now have better medicines. In the case of the Foxglove our modern remedies for heart failure in particular revolve around the cardiac glycosides of which digitalis, derived from the seeds of *Digitalis purpurea*, was the original. A king's order to find out the Foxglove's properties led to the discovery of the potent drug and this now keeps thousands of people alive who otherwise would have died of heart disease. The roots are numerous, long, and slender and give rise to a thick, 60–150cm hairy stem, which is extremely tough and gives rise to the fleshy oval crinkled leaves. During the months from June to September we get a succession of flowers, little tubes about 4×2cm hanging down from the stem, purple (or white) with dots on the inside. The whole of Britain has this plant in hedge banks, woodland, and any non-calcareous soil. By the way, it probably holds more medical secrets because it has been used as a very powerful diuretic (leaves) and as a treatment for pulmonary infection and epilepsy.

   This is a very easy plant to grow because it is so unassuming in its choice of soil and conditions but preferring ordinary soil that does not get *too* dry and a slightly sheltered position. Being a biennial, seeds must be planted every year if you want to keep the flowers going, and this should be done out of doors in April–June. Thin out the seedlings to 30cm in a nursery bed until October, when they should be planted in flowering positions for the next year at about 30cm apart again. If you are lucky enough to be given plants in Spring then plant them immediately. There are commercial breeds of Foxgloves that are 'improved' but really the difference is not great and the old wild type still beats them all.

The Common Mallow. *Malva sylvestris.*
   Biennial or perennial. Herbaceous. Any soil except perhaps clay.
This mallow is the one that almost everyone will have seen at one time or another and that justifies its name as being common. A fairly tall (30–91cm) plant, it grows bushy early with large coarse and not unlike the shape of sycamore leaves. It flowers from June–September with a con-tinuous show of large (50mm) flowers. There are five 'inverted heart' pink petals with bracts separating them and with darker pink veining. The blooms come out in a succession and it is due to this that it has a long flowering period but with maybe only a few of the total out at any one

time, though it will make a lovely show despite this. The name *sylvestris* is not really representative of its true habitat because it will live almost anywhere and will make its home on any type of soil though clay is found to be a little more difficult. England and Wales are its main areas but it is spread out all over the country. Some of its local names come from the fact that the seed pod is rather like the shape of a cottage cheese, thus giving us the local names 'cheeses' 'bread and cheese' etc. Its main use medicinally was with the mucilage of the roots, which was used as a poultice, for soothing and as an ointment. Seeds 2.5 × 3cm, kidney shaped. For cultivation see *M. moschata*.

The Musk Mallow. *Malva moschata.*
   Perennial. Herbaceous. A range of soil.
The 'musk' part of the name refers to the smell which is quite musky though not particularly strong. As it is a fairly tall plant (30–61cm) bushy with hairy simple stems and ribbed leaves – a skeleton version of the common variety's leaves. It also flowers from June–September to produce similarly large pink flowers but this time they have petals too large to allow the sight of the green bracts between them. An albino version of this is well known and often cultivated in gardens as also are some of the other deeper coloured forms. The blooms form the same type of succession as those of *sylvestris*, open and close with the sun, and this is the reason that they may often be closed up at a time when you want to look at them. Although they are found all over lowland areas of England and Wales they tend to prefer rich and gravelly soils and are found in much greater abundance and splendour where this is so. (Neutral soil also helps, by the way).
Seeds 2 × 2.5cm, kidney-shaped.
   Naturalization in the United States of America shows just how easy it is to change the habitat of the plant as it now appears over there in huge quantities. Perhaps the Americans make the same use of it as do the French, putting some into tea or sugar as an extra flavouring.
   The method of cultivation is very similar for both species that I have written of here:
   Initial planting can be by transplant from a friend's (rather than God's) garden. It takes easily as long as a fairly warm spot is chosen, and once established it should be left well alone because it doesn't take too kindly to irritation. Lifting and dividing can be done in autumn though it might be better to just throw the unwanted parts away because new cuttings will easily take in sand and they grow rapidly to a nice new plant, so removing the need to disturb the old plant.
   Seeds can be sown in autumn under glass, this producing an earlier start to growth in spring, or they can be planted out of doors in any reasonable soil in spring where they are to flower. Cover the seeds lightly, and store them in the greenhouse. They flower in their 2nd season.
   Problems not to run into are: *Fungi* – I suggest spraying, though they will live through it and it may even be better just to grow new plants. *Spreading* – Not pernicious spreaders but they gangle a bit when put in a dark spot.

Primrose. *Primula vulgaris.*
   Perennial. Moist, humus soil.
An absolute gem for the garden, perfect in almost every degree, well known, common, but decreasing all the time. As a boy I lived in a little

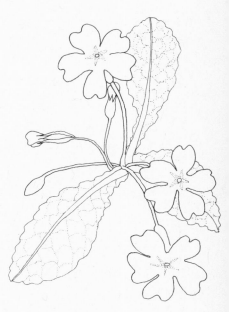

village in Surrey which was well provided with copses and hedgerows in which the primrose abounded. Now, when I go back there are none to be found except in small patchy places – and all this is due to the effect of them being too beautiful to be resisted, and picked or dug up. *Please do not take them from the wild* – it takes many years for a plant to be replaced and they are readily available from florists or nurserymen. From a rosette of oval, crinkly leaves grow many 4–8cm hairy reddish flowering scapes with a massive 3cm brilliant yellow, five petalled flower each. Late March to mid-May sees them blooming in shady, moist deciduous woodland all over Great Britain. This is one of our countryside's great delights and is easy to grow.

For cultivation see Oxslip.

Cowslip. *Primula veris.*
  Perennial. Calcereous or clay soil.
This is very similar to the primrose except that it has a single flowering stem headed by a cluster of 10 or so fatter 'necked', smaller, darker petalled drooped flowers, which come out in succession to give a long blooming period through April and May. It can be found in meadows on chalk, limestone or clay in England and Wales – for some reason it stops at the Scottish border. It quite likes good sunlight and will put up with not quite so rich soil. Cultivation is detailed under Oxslip.

Oxslip. *Primula elatior.*
  Perennial. Calcareous or clay soil.
Very much like a cross between the Primrose and Cowslip with one flowering stem and a series of primrose flowers usually erectly branching from the top. For some reason it is found only in the moist woodland of East Anglia – this explaining why so few people have seen one, though I expect it will grow happily elsewhere. Flowering is in April and May.

A small mention for the Bird's-eye Primrose should be made here because it looks slightly like a pink version of the Oxslip, though it is smaller and grows in northern mountain grassland.

The cultivation of Primulacea does not include taking them from the wild because they do not take particularly well to being put into 'foreign' soil, which, if not rich enough, will merely take up all the minerals from the soil that it brought with the plant and gradually it will die. A much better way is to get examples from the nurseryman and set them in good rich soil in a damp, shady place. The 'slip' part of Oxslip and Cowslip show that these have a predilection for ground with 'ox' or 'cow' dung in abundance. The 1.5mm brown seeds should be planted in rich soil in a slightly heated greenhouse in February or March (or later, out of doors). The reason to get them going as quickly as possible is so that they will be fairly well-developed by the following autumn and flower the following year. Seeds can also germinate in the autumn after being produced – this giving a head start, but if it does not work then the winter frost will set them going as soon as the temperature rises slightly. Divide plants when they get overcrowded but do not let them get too old or run out of rich soil because they will grow straggly and not flower so well.

Great Mullein. Common Mullein. *Verbascum thapsus.*
  Biennial. A tall herb. Dry, stony soil.
Often called Aaron's Rod it grows a tall (30–90cm) winged, leafy, rough stem to be headed by a leash of tight large buds. From June to August

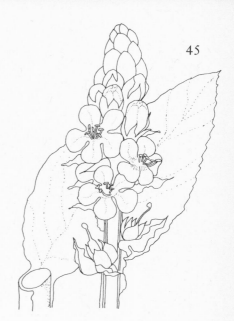

these burst to release the one inch, bright yellow, flowers all the way up the 45cm terminal inflorescence in no particular order giving it a good, bright show for about a month. Five petals, five stamens, and an absence of scent allow it to produce seeds, 1.0 × 0.7mm which are dark grey. This is common in dry, often chalky or gravelly soil in southern England and has been introduced into the States, where it is a garden plant. We, however, do not appear to have realized its ease of growth and beauty yet, despite having been the exporters. The plant was thought to have the power to keep away evil or danger and medicinally it was used for coughs, gripes, piles and many more ailments.

It is distributed widely over many well drained substrates in the South of England. New seeds have to be planted every year in early summer, in well drained (especially chalky) soil and thinned out to 15cm apart when large enough. They should be planted in a sunny spot of a warm part of the garden and transplanted again in autumn to the place where they are to flower the following year (again a warm, sunny, well drained spot without an acid soil). If the ground around it is made dry and hard, then it will grow beautifully but other weeds will not although it makes a very handsome plant whatever the surroundings. Protect from frost if possible.

Dark Mullein. *Verbascum nigrum.*
Biennial. A tall herb. Chalky soil.
This is very similar to but much less showy than its greater cousin, with darker flowers and a shorter stem (30cm).
The culture is very similar to that of *Verbascum thapsus,* though it prefers life to be slightly damper.

Common Toadflax. *Linaria vulgaris.*
Perennial. Any light soil.
An erect plant growing generally in clumps with 5cm lanceolate leaves coming off the stem at right angles and a head of light yellow snapdragons at the top, each of them about 10mm across. It is scentless; is it largely hairless as well so it is a useful bedding plant found all over the south-east of England.

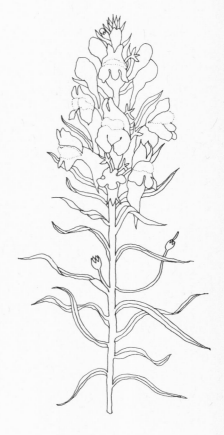

It may only grow 15cm tall, but that spike is stacked with flowers, which completely outshine the leaves and make a patch incredibly striking. There are few plants I know of, including much famed garden varieties, that can beat it for sheer density of flower colour and it is surely an excellent candidate for even the fussiest gardener's beds. It has only one drawback – it spreads quickly so hem it in with Mint or Vetch and that wandering propensity will soon cease. The horticulture behind a successful gardenful of this is shared with the other species of Linaria though they each have a few peculiarities. Planting can take place in Spring or Autumn as small clumps about a foot apart – in light, well-drained soil and a sunny position. That sun is necessary, by the way, so if you live far north then perhaps there will be some difficulty. Division of the stock can take place in Autumn or Spring and the minute seeds can be planted in September for late Spring flowering or April for Summer flowering. Germination is very fast and should take place where they are to bloom and very lightly covered if at all. There are many annual varieties of Linaria, but we are lucky enough in Britain to have just perennials so let's make the most of it. Linaria Purpurea should be treated similarly.

Purple Toadflax. *Linaria purpurea.*
 Perennial. Any light soil.
Growing 5–8cm high with a straight stem and greyish leaves coming off it all the way up to the spike of purple snapdragon (except, like Common Toadflax they have a spur as a neck for the dragon) flowers. It is found on waste ground, and roughwalls, in Southern England fairly commonly.

Creeping Toadflax. *Linaria repens.*
 Perennial. Dryish soil.
Very much like the others except that the stem starts off by being decumbent then turns skywards to give off at its tip the familiar-shape flowers, but this time only streaked with purple (although there is a white version of it).
 It is found towards the west, especially in the new county of Dyfed, and flowers in June and August.

THE FORGET-ME-NOTS

They are all very similar in shape, flower, and size but each one has its very different ecological niche and it is at times like this that the importance of ecology in gardening becomes obvious. I will detail three plants, all of them common but each confined to its own little stratum of plant society. There are very many, slightly more demanding, species of Forget-me-not with similar methods behind their cultivation but they are generally not as abundant as these.

Water Forget-me-not. *Myosotis palustris.*
 Perennial. Water edges.
Rather straggly compared to the others, it sends out many 12–24cm stems from its creeping base, each with a terminal of beautiful blue or, rarely white flowers. The small (1.5 × 1.0mm) nutlets (4 per flower) can be used to propagate in the way shown below or, rather simpler the rooting side-shoots can be detached and planted separately. The best shows I have seen of this were in Essex lining a river with blue, though it grows all over the country in wet shady places.

Common Forget-me-not. *Myosotis arvensis.*
 Annual. Any soil.
The myosotis name of the genus comes from 'ear of a mouse' probably from the shape of the petals, which are beautifully rounded. There are many colours and varieties of this that the seedsmen put out and, to give them their due, they produce excellent flowery plants. In the wild it can be found almost as a by-product of agriculture around field edges and on waste ground. Descriptions of this 6cm plant I feel are unnecessary except to say that the exquisitely curved flowering stem gradually straightens through the flowering season (the entire summer).

Wood Forget-me-not. *Myosotis sylvatica.*
 Short lived Perennial. Moist woodland soil.
This grows as one of the herbs of woodland with a decumbent, leaf rosetted, often rooting base to its 12–24cm, hairy-leaved flowering branched stem. Masses of the unusually large (up to 1cm across) flowers crowd together as a beautiful blue or rarely white cluster at the stemhead from May to July.

The only problem with it is that it is the rarest – though still locally common one of the three preferring the North of England, Midlands and South East.

It is bound to be able to put up with lower light levels, and more acid soil than the other two so give it a good, moist, shady position.

The annual varieties should have their seeds planted, where they are to bloom in March and thinned to about 12–16cm apart or as necessary. Perennials are better grown as biennials, seeds (usually 1.5 × 1.0mm dark brown) being sown out of doors, ½in deep in summer in rich ordinary soil, sheltered from the midday sun and separated 6–8ins apart. That should be done in a nursery bed, transplantation taking place the following spring to the flowering position. If you do not want to have to go to the trouble of collecting seeds laboriously then the withering flowered plants can be set back in the nursery border and allowed to self sow, which happens readily.

GERANIUMS

All of us have heard of Geraniums but many people seem to think that they are purely garden flowers. Their name, in fact, comes from the latin *geranos* (a crane) and by some strange coincidence the wild types have as their popular names the Cranesbills. So you see this popular garden group can be traced back to its wild beginnings by its name.

Most of them are very similar in configuration and horticultural properties so, apart from a few notes with each one, the gardening procedure is after the last of them.

Herb Robert. *Geranium robertianum.*
Perennial. Dry, perhaps calcareous soil, though any should do.
Known to all, this little flower, with its five petals and low bushy foliage, peeps out at you from the depths of its leaves. A delicate, beautiful small flower, though perhaps I am a little biased about it because it brings back memories of the countryside so well. Unfortunately it has an almost unpleasant smell and the flowers are rather small, being only 1cm across and at least in pairs. Flowers all summer from May to the end of September. Well known throughout the country for its association with goblins. Does this account for it being my favourite flower?

It should go fairly well by the standard horticulture for geraniums. Normally it has a habitat of shady woodland and fertile, damp soil, in which its seed should be planted just after collection or in October to flower the following year. Note that it is an annual so that all the propagation procedures for the others can be ignored; anyway the seeds are good.

Bloody Cranesbill. *Geranium sanguineum.*
Perennial. Limey or sandy soil.
Certainly a great flower to have. From a tough creeping rhizome comes the hairy vertical stem (there is also a trailing version) carrying hairy 'skeleton' leaves, and at the top a large (about 2cm) bloom. Usually there is only one flower out at any one time. The five rounded petals are either a bright red or a bleached white, coming out in June, July and August. Coastal areas seem to get an extremely large share of its population particularly in the North, growing as it does in rocky places, in chalk and limestone soils – it should be noted that poor soils are needed to be able to control its growth.

Dusky Cranesbill. *Geranium phaeum.*
    Perennial. Slightly acid soil.
A flower introduced to Britain perhaps for its large (2cm) paired flowers, which vary in colour from a deep purple to almost black. Woody stock gives rise to a 22–50cm stem carrying the large rounded leaves and a head of the few May to July flowers. It will hybridize with the very similar (in many ways) *Geranium pratense* to produce many different strains and just like it, the flower heads must be removed before they seed because the bursting capsule scatters the seeds far and wide, ruining any tidy gardening policy. Both of these species are getting rather rare in their normal habitat of damp meadows and woods of lowland Central Britain and could do with a little help from us to boost the numbers. After all, they are extremely attractive.

Meadow Cranesbill. *Geranium pratense.*
    Perennial. Limey soil.
Perhaps this, the most common of the Cranesbills, should be regarded as a garden plant only of those gardeners who have considerable skill, because it is in my view a plant that is difficult to please, and spreads its seeds far and wide, if the capsule is left on. Pastures, thickets, basic soils, all over the country except Devon, Cornwall and North West Scotland have a propensity for growing it, but it appears to prefer limestone formations of England.
    Growing 30–60cm tall, from thick, ruddy rootstock, it is very reminiscent of a buttercup in its stem and foliage appearance, but bears a succession of pretty 4cm blue, five-petalled flowers from early June to late August.

Wood Cranesbill. *Geranium sylvaticum.*
    Perennial. Damp soil.
It is a shame that it is difficult to grow deliberately, because having a greater number of flowers and fewer leaves than its Common relative, it is extremely attractive. The woody stock, found in damp woods especially in the North Riding of Yorkshire and northwards, gives a slender branching stem 30cm tall with delicate leaves and numerous paired, blue/purple flowers during the period from late May to early June.

    Please look at the individual habitat detailed under each plant and change the conditions of growth to fit that.
    All the types can be planted between October and March, ready for the year's growth. A well-drained position in sun or partial shade should suffice, though often full shade is the natural home of the plant. Division of roots can be done in spring or autumn and this is a fairly convenient method which provides good plants. Their eventual size should dictate how far apart they should be planted e.g. 30cm for *Geranium robertianum* and 45cm for *Geranium sanguinium*.
    Cuttings of new growth shoots can be taken in spring, because they will root easily in sand and fill out well enough by the following autumn, so as not to need protection during the winter. Seed sowing does not need the complicated mixtures of loam, peat, sand etc. that gardening magazines are forever prescribing, it just needs ordinary soil, outside or perhaps under glass, in early spring. If you can bear to put up with keeping the soil fairly clear over the winter, the best method is to plant the 4 × 2mm seeds about 1cm down in autumn and just wait until they come up in the spring. There is a very good germination rate, so that you should be able to guarantee

a plant from each seed. One of the pointless horticultural arguments among the professionals is concerned with whether or not to feed wild geraniums before flowering. Answer: it will help in poor soils but not in rich ones, and by that time the plant should have decided the number of flowers already, so in the interests of economy and leisure – don't bother! If a drought hits the garden, they will be one of the first to need a drink.

Red Campion. *Silene dioica.*
    Annual or short living perennial. Herbaceous. Any soil.
This plant puts out a slightly branched 30–90cm stem from a short creeping base. The stem is clad with hairy lanceolate leaves that, in good soil may make it rather bushy, and is topped by an inflorescence of five-petalled, white eyed pink flowers which come out in turn to provide a good flowering period (April–August). The seeds (1.3mm kidney shaped or round, black) can be taken from the capsule once it has dried in the same way as collecting poppy seeds and this can be done usually in September.
For some odd reason it seems to be put together, in the mind of the early Englishman, with the bluebell and the early purple orchid which grow in roughly the same localities and have the same common name in some areas. It is found all over Great Britain, except the Scottish highlands and the fenlands, but especially along with the agricultural areas as it seems to have been introduced by invading farmers and spread inland with them. Woods, shady places, and hedgerows are its favourite haunts.
    The method of enticing this beauty into your parlour is described under Ragged Robin as they are very similar plants.

White Campion. *Silene alba.*
    Generally a perennial. Herbaceous. Any soil.
This plant is very much like its red friend except that it is hairier and white, of course, in its flowers. It inhabits the same areas and does all the same things except that it likes a little more warmth and congregates towards the South-East of the country more than the red variety. Just to be difficult there is a white version of the Red Campion and there are rather neat ways of detecting that it is not really a white Red Campion, *viz.* White Campion opens towards evening and exudes a strong scent whereas the red and its albino open during the day and are scentless. The legend associated with this plant are interesting, if a little macabre: pick a red and it kills your father whereas pick a white and it kills your mother.
    There are separate male and female plants. You will see that the Red and White Campions are almost indistinguishable anatomically, and the same is true horticulturally, so they are both dealt with after Ragged Robin.

Ragged Robin. *Lychnis flos-cuculi.*
    Perennial. Herbaceous. Any damp soil.
At one time it was and still is, to some extent, grown in gardens. And very rightly too, for its handsome ragged red flowers and neat stem are lovely. The tapering fibrous brown rootstock that is perennial each year sends up a new flowering stem about 45cm tall with a few sticky leaves, only the lower ones being stalked. Of the 'pink' family it gives handsome five-petalled flowers not unlike those of the Campion but with a much more frayed-looking edge and giving the whole plant a rather fiery look. Flowers bloom in succession during early summer and release the small black kidney-shaped seeds soon after flowering finishes. It is common all

over Great Britain except the Wash area and is quite happy in any soil. Slightly scented.

These are generally annual flowers, and those that survive into subsequent years may not be quite as handsome as their short lived relatives, so it is probably a good idea to plant by seed a new set each year; to increase the stock this is necessary as vegetative methods are not good.

The seeds can be planted in moisture-retentive, though well drained, ordinary soil either in March under glass, lightly covered and about 5 cm apart or outside in April where they are to flower. (Move those seedlings that are in the cold frame to their flowering site when about 10 cm. tall). To get an earlier show the seeds can be sown out of doors in October and left to winter in the ground. They will spring up as soon as possible past winter but the frost may get them that way so make it a fairly well sheltered spot. As a border, masses should be planted with maybe only 5cm between them.

The following three species all belong to the genus Silene under 1 classification and so their horticulture is very similar and I will deal with them together under Bladder Campion.

Sea Campion. *Silene maritima.*
Perennial. Woody, bushy. Any soil.
This is really one to recommend in that it has an easily containable creeping woody stem which sends out a sort of bushy, highly flowered set of shoots to produce a clump of brilliant white; the flowers being much like the other Campions. The leaves are shorter and lighter, however, being dwarfed by the flowers, which get to be 2cm in diameter and stick out to make it about 20cm tall. It is found all over our coast and is pretty hardy as it managed to get through the last ice age and not need re-introduction.

Nottingham Catchfly. *Silene nutans.*
Perennial. Dry, stony soil.
This is rather rare and I must ask you if you find it not to dig it up in the hope that it will root in the garden, as its seeds are quite good enough to get it back to the old homestead. 30–60cm high, it is sticky towards the top, white flowers with deeply divided petals in a sort of grasping shape, coming out late June to mid-August, a bit smaller in every dimension than the others and with smaller seeds.

Found on sea cliffs, dry places particularly in Cheshire and Derbyshire and on cliffs.

Bladder Campion. *Silene vulgaris.*
Perennial. Not soil fussy.
This rather withered looking plant got its name from the bladders that are left behind after the flower has gone and contain the ripening seed. It has the same type of perenation as the others in that the underground roots send out a new flowering stem every year but it is different in that in this case that stem and its leaves are hairless and deeply veined. The flowers which arrive above the leaves come from the stem separate from the leaf axils (unlike the Red or White Campions) and have much more firmly divided petals.

It is a beautiful plant, easy to grow and excellent for the rockery.

All these perennials can be planted in autumn or spring in well drained places with plenty of water available. A sandy loam mixed with well-rotted leaf mould will receive it well and also acts as the substrate for seeds and cuttings. Division in spring (early April usually) produces good results as does the production of cuttings of young shoots in July. Seeds can be sown in pans (not necessary for Sea Campion) under glass in March–April and about 2cm apart to bloom in the first year after planting out in sunny positions about 7cm tall.

Autumn Crocus. *Crocus nudiflorus.*
  Perennial. Damp pastures.
This is very similar in many ways to the Saffron, flowering after the leaves, during Autumn, and producing the same shaped parts, but the leaves have a white stripe down the centre and often many flowers are produced in succession, being purple or purpley blue. It is also shorter, its flowers being a mere 10–15cm and its leaves 10–20cm and produces long, strong scaly runners, which will spread it slowly around the garden if left alone. Being a naturalized foreign plant, its main concentration here is in the areas of the great gardens of the eighteenth century, though it is now becoming rare around the Manchester area where it used to be quite common.
  Cultivation is similar to the Meadow Saffron.

Naked Ladies or the Meadow Saffron. *Colchcum autumnale.*
  Perennial. Basic soils.
Very much like the crocus this plant perennates in exactly the same way, by corm. From the corm modern science has been able to extract a very powerful substance medicinally, known as colchicine which is now used in the treatment of gout and cancer but is extremely poisonous in even small quantities and it was for that reason that for many years it was hated and associated with death. I do not think a potted description will help much because everyone knows just what a crocus looks like but suffice it to say that it may come in purplish, reddish or white colours, the purple being the most common, and that it sends up 10–20cm flower, the petals of which open very wide, and some thick strong leaves. It flowers from early August to late September in its normal habitat of damp fields and open limey pasture and it flowers after the leaves have gone. The areas in which it was once cultivated, i.e. Gloucester and Oxford, are now the places where it is still found most abundantly.
  The ground around the crocus is bound at sometime to get infested with weeds so may I suggest that it is 'underplanted' by being put into soil that already holds something undemanding like Thyme or grass. Remember if you do this, that the grass must not be cut until the leaves have died down because the corm needs the goodness of its foliage to swell properly for the next year's growth. Planting should be in July and August in rich, moist soil, a few inches apart, and in a good light spot. Split the clumps of offsets at the same time and every three years. If you feel it is worthwhile and want quicker growth, sow seeds in a rich loam-and-humus mixture in August and September 3mm deep in a cold frame and plant out in the permanent site when 2 years old. If you have got inquisitive children in the house then do not let them taste the corm. Colchicine is a killer. If you would like a Christmas flower show then just follow the same regime as with the Bluebell, convincing the corm that spring has arrived.

Pasque Flower. Danes Blood. *Anemone pulsatilla.*
  Perennial. Light chalky soil.
A really beautiful flower, and of course a rare one, so please do not go out

52

and deplete the meagre stocks that are left in isolated areas, but let it build up to beautify much greater ones. It only grows 10–20cm high but in that short space it manages to put in along its silky stem a number of bristly leaves and usually one huge 30–35mm purple, seven petalled (yellow-eyed) flower on a short stalk. The flower is hairy too in its blooming period from the middle of April to the end of May and has a slight scent. It usually grows on chalk grassland with a thick vertical rootstock but it will make do with lime and mortar rubble if given the chance.

Plant it in October or March in light loamy soil and in a generally sunny place. There is controversy about its favourite soil, some people say pH 6.5 and others insist that lime is best, but probably it is of little significance with just good drainage as the only prerequisite. Seeds will go best if planted out of doors, 1cm down as soon as they are ripe and that soil guarded from weeds until the following year.

PAPAVERACEAE. POPPY FAMILY

Yellow Horned Poppy. *Glaucium flavum.*
Biennial. Sandy soil.
Found particularly on English and eastern Irish sea coasts it is a silvery looking plant growing from 30–60cm tall with thickish stems, which give a yellow juice when bruised. The scentless 6cm pale-yellow flowers come out from June to September to produce long honeycombed black seeds in pods.

Plant autumn or spring in sandy, moist soil in an open position. To keep a good display going it will be necessary to create new plants every year and this is best done by sowing seeds 1cm deep in sandy soil out of doors in late April or May, spreading them 15cm apart when large enough to resist damage and then moving them to their final site in autumn or the following spring to bloom in that year. A very attractive flower, giving huge, long seed pods and making the autumn seed collection easy.

Welsh Poppy. *Meconopsis cambrica.*
Perennial. Ordinary soil.
It is nice to find that a native flower can rival all the foreign types and here is a perfect example; a pretty flower 30–60cm up on its foliated stem. The tapering rootstock sends up a few light green hairy leaves and the flower, which is 30–40mm across and a brilliant yellow despite many of its genus being red and blue (and Asian as well). There are orange forms; it is scentless and ends up after its June, July and August flowering range as a long pod of minute black seeds. Not surprisingly it is found most often in moist shady places in Wales particularly and North Devon.

The tiny, oval, black seeds can be planted in autumn as soon as they are ripe, in boxes about 2cm apart. Leave them in the greenhouse in their well-rotted leaf mould soil until they germinate in the spring when they should be hardened off, separated to about 10cm and planted out in a sheltered place. Water them generously in summer and leave them dry in winter, because then all the moisture will do is encourage their enemies. Do not worry about having more the next year because it self seeds well. *Do not go out and dig up wild plants because they do not transplant well.* A little protection from rampant weeds will be necessary at first but eventually it should dominate its place.

Field Poppy. *Papaver rhoeas.*

Annual. Light, loamy soil.

Surprisingly this plant is poisonous, with its 45cm hairy flowering scapes leading to the familiar, Flanders, red, four-petalled poppy, and its feathery leaves around the base. It is found in light soil throughout Britain and produces copious amounts of very small kidney shaped brown seeds. Take care! It is a plant protected by the corn gods and, picking it brings on thunder and danger.

Usually if a 'garden' type Poppy flower is allowed to seed then over successive years the offspring will be found to have reverted to the old papaver type. The process of allowing it to stay in the bed and letting it seed will produce many more plants the following year, simply by fallen seed, and this shows just how easy it is to grow. Sow seeds out of doors, where they are to bloom the following year, as soon as they are ripe or in late August. There will be high seed losses over the winter in areas of heavy soil though this may be alleviated by breaking it up with compost. Thin the seedlings as they grow in March and April until the remaining plants are 16–20cm apart and just leave them to bloom. If a fading flower head is taken off (they certainly do not last long) often this will encourage further production and prolong the season.

VIOLETS

The one thing I should say before I start is that they are all in exactly the same shape and almost the same size so I will give a detailed description of one of them and merely note the ways in which the others vary.

It is a fascinating group of flowers with all the varieties one could wish for, and in all the circumstances one could want. A species for everyone.

Dog Violet. *Viola riviniana.*

Perennial. Fertile, rich soil.

A low plant growing from a woody stem up to about 15cm above the ground as a branching stem with spade- (playing-card spade, that is) shaped leaves coming off at irregular intervals and long flower stalks carrying the purple- (or, of course, violet-) coloured flowers. It is found all over Great Britain, though it prefers the warm and wet south-west areas; it likes woods, hedge margins, and damp meadows and it attracts bees in search of its nectar, which is situated at the back of the tubular flower base.

Heartsease. *Viola tricolor.*

Perennial, or annual depending on the variety. Ordinary, light soil.

Locally common throughout the nation on arable land occurring as a little bushy plant with flowers of purple and yellow petals or just yellow ones.

There are not really that many flowers to warrant it being grown as a border plant, but I'm sure that it would be useful for breeding. It flowers throughout the summer. It is shorter lived than the others but resows itself.

Mountain Pansy. *Viola lutea.*

Perennial. Basic soils.

Difficult to grow in the garden but rewarding if you can because the flowers are larger and may be any shade between yellow and blue (flowering between June and August). Highland or just hilly moorland is its habitat.

Sweet Violet. *Viola odorata.*
Perennial. Ordinary soil.

The great thing here is the scent, which though not strong is very attractive. The stem has few branches, it flowers during early spring, and then possibly again in the autumn, it has woody stock, and it likes hedgebanks and woods but otherwise it is very similar to the Dog Violet. Beware! Long runners!

The symbol of Ancient Athens, the famous present from Napoleon to his Josephine, an object of praise from Francis Bacon, Shakespeare and many more, in fact, throughout the ages this must have been one of the most complimented of British flowers with medicinal and herbal uses to add to its beauty. Up to landscape garden times it was a very popular garden plant, but since then it has drifted into disuse. What a waste!

Marsh or Bog Violet. *Viola palustris.*
Perennial. Rich soil in damp places, acid.

Bogs and marshes are the haunts of this dwarf version of the others. Other differences include much more rounded leaves, pinker petals, and the flower stalks coming from the short underground stem. Early summer gets it out in force.

Each of the Violets has slightly differing requirements so try and adapt the methods I have outlined below to fit the plant in question more exactly.

Transplanting can be done in any season provided that a good ball of soil is taken with it, and the new site has humus-filled soil, acidic if anything with partial shade or an easterly aspect. Divide after flowering or, for those clump-forming plants, in spring. Cuttings can be taken in summer and put in sand to root before planting them out again. The question as to how the 2×1.5mm seeds should be raised has many answers, but my favourite involves sowing them fresh in July and August out of doors, or in frames and transplanting to where they are to flower in the following spring. The soil for this should be very good to make sure that sufficient growth is made to get the plant through the winter. If you live in a warm part of the country, perhaps seed planting in a heated frame in January or February would achieve the same results, but the previous method I think would be less bother. The problem of collecting seeds is not inconsiderable because they are dropped so quickly and the answer seems to be to search early or look around the base of the plant, where there is often some lying quite obvious.

For winter flowering plant in September in 15cm pots and make sure the temperature around it stays above 8°C or plant it in 13°C heated sand, at about the usual 10cm apart. Pinch off side runners to produce bigger flowers in the following spring, pick off the dying, spent flowers, and do not over water; also keep fairly weed free, because they cannot win battles of supremacy against even moderately aggressive opponents.

Cornflower or Bluebottle. *Centaurea cyanus.*
Annual. Arable soil.

This relative of the Knapweeds is similarly spread through Europe – the Kaiser's favourite flower, many French remedies, etc., but here in Britain it made ink but gained ill-repute from its ability to blunt the sickle with its woody stem when the corn was harvested. For that reason it was driven out from arable areas of Britain and has not returned, so it is found occasionally on arable land and waste places in lowland Britain. It grows as a slight, woody branching stem 30–60cm tall topped from mid-July to early September by the flat 3–5cm flowers. These are blue (possibly white or pink or double) multi-petalled affairs with prominent black anthers. The flowers fade to leave a pappus which should be removed if you want to stop it spreading.

Sow the 6 × 3mm white achenes in autumn (for the best results) or early spring where they are to flower, in rich soil (adding a little fertilizer to make sure), and thin to 12cm apart. This should be in a sunny place and protected from the wind.

Lesser Periwinkle. *Vinca minor.*
Perennial. Ordinary soil.

The name 'vinca' comes from the latin 'to bind' which shows just how good it is at encroaching on other plants in its trailing, evergreen manner. Creeping stock, rooting at nodes, and giving off shiny, paired leaves, sprouts erect 10–15cm stems in its first year, that give attractive lilac five-petalled flowers, about 2cm across, in spring and early summer. In France it is an emblem of the pleasures of memory and of sincere friendship and here in Britain it is a symbol of love and fertility. Medicinally it was used as a cure for cramp and as a general heal-all, which gave it one of its local names. Southern England accounts for the most part of the British population, it being found in warm, light localities of woods, thickets, copses and the like.

This plant and the Greater Periwinkle have similar methods of culture.

Greater Periwinkle. *Vinca major.*

This is similar in most ways to the Lesser Periwinkle, except that it grows even further than Lesser Periwinkle, trails and rambles more, and is generally bigger, and has yellow hairy sepals.

Eventually both this species and the Lesser Periwinkle, which is the more suitable as a border plant, will form a good evergreen ground cover so plant them in November or March in ordinary soil, in sun or dry shade in a space that needs covering. A useful combination is Vinca and Primulacae, the two going together very well indeed and excluding most unwanteds. Propagation is either by cuttings taken in the late summer of non-flowering new running stems and set in sand in a cool greenhouse to root or by division done in autumn or spring. The shoots root as they go and the best method is to divide by simply cutting the shoots up into separately rooted pieces. Clipping off the short tips will encourage the formation of a bushier plant and may improve the flowering properties.

HYPERICUMS

This name is well known to gardeners already through the many, mainly foreign breeds that we grow, plants such as Rose of Sharon, certainly deserve a place. Here, however are some rarer wild ones:

Common St John's Wort. *Hypericum perforatum.*
Perennial. Non-calcareous ordinary soil.

The rituals and properties which surround this are the most striking I have seen: it was used to treat wounds, to prevent the entry of demons to a household, to raise spirits, and many more. St John's day is the 24 June and this is where the name comes from. On the morning of the 23rd, before the sun has risen, the flowers were picked and that evening they were smoked over

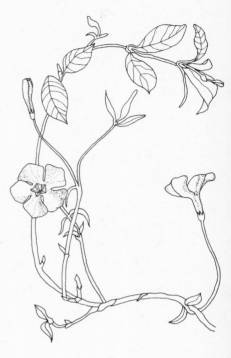

a fire to intensify the exorcising properties for the following day. Christianity adopted this ritual but no one knows just how long it had been around before that time. It grows from tufted, woody, creeping roots a ribbed, square stem that, when bruised, often gives out a red liquid and perhaps it is from this that the homeopathic treatment of bleeding has arisen. The leaves are about 2cm long, with pellucid dots on them, which exude an aromatic oil. The substances involved here are fluorescent and sensitize cow's skin to light, causing it to become inflamed. As a cluster at the head of each branching shoot, are a number of 1.5cm yellow, five-petalled flowers with black dots on the petals, three stigmas (often crimson) and many obvious tufty stamens. These flowers can be seen from July to September and were once gathered to make a yellow wool dye. It is found mainly in south-east England in fairly damp, not too hilly, grassland or thicket. There are many plants of this genus in Britain and all of them can be recommended for their particular habitat.

Slender St John's Wort. *Hypericum pulchrum.* Slim. Non calcareous soils.

Hairy St John's Wort. *Hypericum hirsutum.* Shady places.

Tutsan. *Hypericum androsaemum.* A bushy plant.
They have a similar culture method of planting – October to March in a fairly damp but light place (actually this varies very much with species) except Tutsan, which should be planted in March or April. In late Spring cuttings can be taken of young shoots or in April seeds (often 0.8 × 0.3mm cylindrical and pointed) can be sown outdoors in a sunny spot and thinned as necessary. Dislike lime soil.

Bluebell. *Endymion nonscriptus.*
   Perennial. Slightly acid soil.
Throughout recorded history, the one thing that the Bluebell is noted for is its commonness, and despite hordes of school children picking armsful of them, this still remains one of the commonest flowers in Britain and one of which we should be proud. A stout, scaly bulb often very deeply inserted into the soil, sends up numerous long thin shiny leaves as a rosette around the hollow 30–45cm stem that exudes a white juice and holds the bell-shaped flowers as a dense terminal raceme. Blue, or rarer, pink or white flowers hang from the stalk, flowering after maturing, one after another from April to late May and carpet the leafless deciduous woods of almost every part of Britain with an attractive sweet-smelling layer. If you get really fed up with the way they keep coming back every year, in places they are not wanted, then perhaps you will feel like making glue or starch out of the bulbs as was done in the Middle Ages, but they can be discouraged more easily by repeatedly removing their leaves or by digging them up.
   Plant the bulb in a pot containing well-rotted leaf mould or fibre, with a drainage bottom to it, and plant it deep because this is what the bulb is used to in the wild. Water it thoroughly, put it in a cool dark place for eight weeks (bulb 'thinks' it is winter) and then gradually increase the light and temperature to 18° or so (spring) where upon it should sprout and flower. Once the flowers have withered, feed the leafy remains and lift the bulb once the leaves have withered.
   So for next Christmas, plant the bulbs in August and September. In the garden, plant the bulbs in autumn or winter at about 7–15cm below the

surface of the rich soil, lift and take off the offset bulbs in summer and feed the soil because they take a lot out. Remember they flower before trees come into leaf, so you can plant them in woodland.

Globe Flower. *Trollius europaeus.*
   Perennial. Ordinary to heavy soil.
The name comes from the shape of the flower, which, without sepals manages to curl up into a light yellow ball with only a small opening for the pollinators to enter. An uncommon plant, it grows on damp pastures, woods, hilly areas and uplands basically in the Scottish West Highlands and the hills of North England and North Wales. The numerous tightly branched flowering stems grow from a strong fibrous stock making it a good candidate for cultivation in gardens and indeed it could be found there in the 1840s.

   Planting can take place in moist, humus-rich deep soil, in October in a waterside or damp place in full or semi-sun. Division can take place as soon as the clump has attained a size too great for liking, or every 3–4 years. Spring or autumn are both pretty good times for this as they are for sowing seeds in rich loam under glass. The seedlings, thinned to 10cm apart should be planted out in late spring, and, by the way, don't worry if your seeds take a long time to germinate because they always do.

BELLFLOWERS

There are many Bellflowers. The list may look a little daunting and, indeed, I couldn't recommend trying them all in a single year, but they are a worthwhile addition to the garden. All of them have roughly the same cultivation methods which I have detailed after the Harebell.

Spreading Bellflower. *Campanula patula.*
   Biennial. Light soil.
A very slight and tender plant with slim stems that branch frequently and produce many yellow-eyed red-petalled flowers at their heads. Each dainty flower is about 2cm across and produces copious numbers of seeds which will mean a quickly spreading bed, unless easy steps are taken against it. I was surprised to learn that such a quickly reproducing plant should be getting rare and confined to the Severn and Wye valleys, for the most part, but the dwindling numbers can be put down to the ease with which they are stopped by other more strongly growing plants. Shady places, woodland margins and similar habitats will see it standing its 45cm and making a splendid show. I have not seen it successfully cultivated here in Britain yet, and I am told that it is difficult, but in Europe it is an easy plant to grow so perhaps it may be so here.

Rampion Bellflower. *Campanula rapunculoides.*
   Perennial. Ordinary soil.
The reason that I include this particularly, is because it was at one time cultivated in gardens, but has gone out of fashion. It is very much like *Campanula patula*, except in that the flowers are smaller and pale blue, being just under 2cm across and in dense terminal racemes to the much less branched stem. It has a fleshy root, which is tuberous, and flowers between early July and early September.

Clustered Bellflower. *Campanula glomerata.*
    Perennial. Chalky soil.
When I say chalky grassland for this plant, I should really point out that it will not grow at all unless there is a good content of lime in the soil. The richer the soil, outside this requirement, then the taller the plant will grow, even up to the point of requiring support, when it gets past 60cm tall. A long stem gives off flowers in ones, up to a very dense cluster (hence the name) of flowers which are a mauve colour, 15mm across and come out from May to September.

    If you are going to have a go with this one, then I should warn you to leave some space for it to grow into, because it likes to increase its patch every year.

Nettle-leaved Bellflower. *Campanula trachelium.*
    Perennial. Heavy soil.
A common plant of woodland and hedgerow of Central, Southern and Eastern England, it grows from 30–90cm tall, with a square stem giving off serrated leaves and a terminal set of lilac bell-shaped flowers. Each one of these blooms is large (about 2cm long) and is formed up by the fusion of the edges of the five petals, giving the characteristic bell with pointed lips, which appears from mid-July to late August. Do not be put off by my saying that the colour of the flowers is just lilac, because there are many wild varieties in a range of colour from blue to white, and there are even double forms. A yellow latex is secreted by the plant and this was used as a treatment for sore throats and tonsilitis.

Giant Bellflower. *Campanula latifolia.*
    Perennial. Any soil but lime preferred.
This time I have been preceded by other horticulturalists, because this is already a garden flower and a very fine one. A stout hairy stem, between 60–120cm tall, supports a number of flowering stems, the flowers themselves and the rough serrated leaves. What to admire here, are their marvellous flowers, which come out from mid-July to early September and are very similar to those of Nettle-leaved Bellflower, in that they are large, blue or white and in a terminal raceme, but different in that they open wider and have many more flowers per stem. Woodland margins and banks provide its home in the North and the Midlands mainly.

Harebell or **Bluebell** in Scotland. *Campanula rotundifolia.*
    Perennial. Dryish soil.
Once again I do not think that there is much need for a detailed description, because it is such a well-known plant, but suffice it to say that from July to September a 15–30cm slightly branched, slender stem with thin leaves will carry a number of 2cm long dainty, light blue flowers. It is found on dry, grassy land, all over Great Britain, except in the Western Peninsula. Parts of the United States have it, due to the action of large supermarket chains giving out the seeds as free gifts, the customers scattering them all over the roadsides, where they now have settled and the fast creeping underground stems ensuring a strong foothold. There are also albino and double versions. Come to think of it, the supermarket had the right idea.

    Plant the perennials in autumn or spring in full sun for the most part, though the woodland varieties should have partial shade. Divide them at the same time and replant in the well broken up, light soil. Those that have extensive creeping roots, can be divided into very many separate plants in autumn, particularly.

Seeds are mostly used to propagate the biennials because they must have fresh plants every year, though the same method is used for all types. Sow the 1.5 × 0.7mm brown seeds, where they are to flower in March, fairly widely spaced, not covered and, ideally, in light moisture-retentive loamy compost. For such a widely varying British set of species, the genus Campanula has not done very well for itself here, except for the Harebell, so I would guess that quite stringent habitat requirements are needed for it to be able to fight off weed competition, so try to keep the plants concentrated or keep weeds away.

Blood-drop Emlets. *Mimulus luteus.*
Perennial. Moist ground.
This is basically similar to *Mimulus gattatus* but it has long, hairless stalks and fewer flowers at a time. The flowers do in fact go on for about four months, so the 2cm blotchy purple flowers do not give you a skimpy show. Originally it was a native of Chile but now it frequents Southern Scotland.

You may have *Mimulus moschatus,* Monkey Musk, in your garden at the moment. This is a native of North America but its musky smell made it a popular addition to English gardens.

The Aleutians must have been a good hardening off bed because it is a 'toughie', putting up with very cold conditions quite easily. A cold corner of the garden where everything else has been discouraged should be suitable, because it is not fussy about the soil.

You can treat it like Monkey Flower in all respects except that its stems root and this means an easy method of propagation by layering.

Cuttings of non-flowering stems can be taken during summer and planted in moist soil until good roots form.

Treat it like Monkey Flower, except remember that it is a *land* plant.

HEATHERS

The use of the Heathers comes in their amazing ability to put up with acid soil and to cover ground so well.

Bell Heather. *Erica cinerea.*
Perennial. Acid soil.
There are dozens of types of this species all of which can be found by wandering around the right areas of mountainous Britain though most of them are pretty localized, and the differences between them may only be the colour of the flowers which, though normally pink, can be anything from white to purple. The woody stem spreads horizontally and gives off the ascending branches up to 60cm high, ending with a cluster of small bell-shaped flowers hanging from the terminal few nodes. The time between March and May will see the 5mm flowers in bloom.

Irish Heath. *Erica mediterranea.*
Perennial. Acid soil.
This is very similar to the Bell Heather but its flowers are slightly taller, carries its flowers only on one side of the stem and blooms from mid-February until early April in profusion, though the season lasts longer than this in a slightly diminished quantity.

Geographically it is localized in the far West of Ireland.

Ling Heather. *Calluna vulgaris*.
    Perennial. Ordinary or acid soil.
This is separated from the others by the fact that it grows in thick springy mats and has shorter, woodier stems leading to a normally one-sided inflorescence of much smaller flowers, in a greater quantity. The toughness of the stems must have been its greatest asset when it came to domestic use as a brush (*calluna* from the Greek 'to brush') being made into rope, beds and roofs. Nutritionally speaking it was a spice for beer and provides some of the best honey available in its season from July to September. Found often with Bell Heather in poor soil, or exposed places all over Britain, except the heavily farmed regions.

Bog Heather. *Erica tetralix*.
    Perennial. Acid soils.
This is a rather shorter version of Bell Heather, having the same configuration but slightly larger bell-shaped flowers coming from the end of the stem rather than at nodes. It flowers from late July to mid-September in mountainous regions and especially in the West of England and Wales.

All the way through this section I have been recommending acid soils for heathers in general but it must be said that they will tolerate lime in the soil (especially *Erica mediterranea*) though this allows the growth of all sorts of competitive plants. This is one reason that heathers are confined to poor soils, cold places and normally unfavourable conditions, because they can put up with it, whereas the faster growing herbs of more reasonable habitat cannot.
    To exclude the possibility of them being overrun I repeat the recommendation of acid soil, peat or leaf mould. Planting should be done deeply in October, March or April, about 30cm apart initially and thinning out as they grow. Naturally they are rather sprawling and will not form the tidy bundles that gardeners usually require unless they are trimmed, after the flowers have gone. Propagation should be by fresh 2cm cuttings of *non* woody new growth and taken in summer (do not use flowering shoots). They will root quickly in sandy peat and can be planted out the following October. Division of plants can be done in October though I do not recommend it as the old, woody parts do not take kindly to gross disturbance. Layering by simply pegging a long stem to the soil can be done in spring. Wait for the soil-touching part to root and then snip off the old shoot from it. Seeds will take a long time to flower after their spring planting out of doors or under glass and lightly covered.

Gladdon, Roast beef plant. *Iris foetidissima*.
    Perennial. Shallow water. Chalky soil.
This is a perennial evergreen, with a rather unpleasant scent (of roast beef from the flowers!) and worse when one of the leaves is bruised. The leaves and stem are roughly the same as the Yellow Flag except that the leaves follow the flower up its stem and the flowering period for the purpley brown flowers is only May to July. A large part of the flower is in fact the styles, which have become large and brown to almost cover over the petals of the two to three flowers per stem. The Gladdon is found mainly in the South of England, where it prefers shady hedgerows, woods and banks in chalky districts.

The seeds, which I hope you will not absolutely need for procreative purposes are in a capsule that is large and brightly coloured, which was once used as a purgative. If planted (in the rich, light soil as soon as shed) they may take an awfully long time to germinate (possibly 18 months) so I would suggest that dividing the offset bulbs from their parents, in winter, would be more effective and this way you will not have to wait at least two years before they flower. Lift and divide the clump July to September.

Wood Avens. Herb Bennet. *Geum urbanum.*
   Perennial. Ordinary soil.
Growing 30–60cm tall, branched and hairy, it is capped by yellow, Rock Rose type, flowers all summer and clothed in broad, toothed leaves. It likes damp and shady places specially woods and was at one time collected from there for its roots, which have a clover like smell and are supposed to guard a house against evil. Found all over Britain, except Northern Scotland.
   Put it in a shady place in autumn or spring, which are also the times to divide it, and give it the benefit of good well-drained soil. Seeds hold the best way to propagate, producing good plants quickly. They can be planted 5cm apart March or April where the plant is to remain or in February under glass, transplanting at the end of March usually. If you manage to get hold of some early seeds it may be possible to plant them immediately – in June say – and get a big enough plant in the autumn to be able to flower early the next year. Thin out as necessary. The flowers are not exactly spectacular, but they are interesting and a pretty addition. If you have heavy soil then you've said goodbye to Herb Bennet because they die in winter in those conditions.

Wood Anemone. *Anemone nemorosa.*
   Perennial. Humus rich soil.
This very slight and weak-looking plant grows up as a thin stem with a few short hairs from a sticklike tuberous root system, throwing out indented, four fingered leaves as it climbs. At the top, well from March to May anyway, are the 25–30mm diameter sixpetalled, white flowers that cap the usual 12cm tall stem with a star that often droops. Normally the flowers have a slightly pinkish tinge, but there are completely pink and light blue varieties of it growing in the wild as well as a double form. It is found the length and breadth of the country in hedgebanks, woods and other shady places, where it can get the sun before the trees gain their leaves.
   Plant a piece of root horizontally in leaf-moulded ordinary soil about 4cm below the surface, in September before it can dry out, and from this start it should spread all the way around the shady (when the trees have foliated that is) patch it was given. I have no confirmed information about culture from seed, although I suspect that sowing in Autumn in the same rich soil (heavy soil should be broken up with sand and compost) should give good results.

Common Valerian. *Valeriana officinalis.*
Perennial. Calcareous soil especially.
This was a medicinal herb especially highly regarded for its uses as a mild sedative, though from the effects that it has on cats which often grub it up and eat the roots (it makes them lose control and become delirious) I think that the drugs that the plant contains are extremely powerful. It was even grown agriculturally at one time (usually by monks) for its herbal

properties; as tea and for essential oil, which keeps the rather unpleasant smell of the plant. Now found, usually growing up to about 90cm tall, in hedgerows, woodland margins and meadows of the chalky and limestone areas of Britain, it produces bobbles of pink flowers at the end of numerous sideshoots to the main stem and at the top, during the height of summer. The flowers are quite pretty but it has rather an excess of foliage, growing from woody, creeping stock and having a straight, vertical stem.

A loamy soil on the chalky side of neutrality serves the plant best, being planted between October and March on pond or stream sides or any moist spot. Sun or partial shade will satisfy it as will a garden where it gets regular watering. Division of roots in spring, or while dormant, seed sown in poor chalky well-drained soil out of doors in April and allowing self seeding are all good ways to increase the stock. This is a really striking plant, reminding one slightly of Cow Parsley in stature, but having a very distinctive flowering style.

Red Valerian. *Centranthus ruber.*
Perennial. Prefers chalky soil.

An escape from the sixteenth century garden it has made itself at home in our green and pleasant land by growing in masses on chalk cliffs, dry banks and coastal areas of south-west Britain. It grows up to 90cm tall from woody roots, which spread at an alarming rate and it gives off fleshy, edible leaves on its way up to the curiously layered inflorescence, which is made up of the flowers on a terminal head of several small shoots. Each individual flower is red (or white) with a 5mm length and a hind spur, which holds the nectar, that the butterflies that are needed to pollinate them want, blooms during the summer months. The massed flowers are extremely striking and certainly deserve a garden place, though I warn you it may be difficult to stop it from spreading.

Plant in autumn or spring in semi-shade (to stop vigorous progress – if you want it fast then give it full sun) and a warm locality because it isn't all that hardy. It will self seed readily but if you need to plant more seeds it should be out of doors in rich loam, thinning as necessary to flower the following year. Problems in its cultivation will be found to increase with latitude and may be very difficult in Scotland where greenhouse wintering will almost definitely be needed.

Sea Lavender. *Limonium vulgare.*
Perennial. Salty ground.

A pretty plant, growing, erect, from a woody stock and a cluster of leaves, a 30cm stem up to a group of small pink/purple five-petalled flowers, which appear from late July to mid-September. These blooms will stay pretty and colourful all winter in the same manner as the everlasting flowers if cut in summer and allowed to dry. Patches, and even acres of it, can be found mainly along the English and Welsh coasts, but particularly concentrated in the Solent and the Thames estuary, i.e. it likes salty muddy areas and salt marshes particularly.

If you have read through the book this far, then you will know what I mean when I say 'usual culture method'. Otherwise: Plant in spring in well drained, lightish soil, spacing them 15–30cm apart and notice that each year that it is left alone, the better and more prolific the show gets. The reason that it grows so well in salty areas is I believe because it has fewer enemies there, so when put into normal soil it may succumb to the invasions of many plants and root diseases, though I have never seen any problem. If you *do* run into difficulty added watering with brine should help. Seeds (7.0 × 1.5mm, brown) should be planted out of doors, lightly covered, in light sandy soil between April and June. They should be 'where to bloom) and in a sunny position. Lift and divide in spring if you have to, take side shoot cuttings for sandy soil anytime in summer and sit back and enjoy the results.

The Common Daisy. *Bellis perennis.*

Perennial. Any soil.

To many traditional gardeners this may be a sign of mis-management but throughout the ages it has always been looked on as the robin of wild flowers, as an emblem of innocence or fidelity and love. The name originally comes from 'day's eye' because of the habit that it has of opening and closing with the sun throughout its long flowering period from March to October.

I certainly do not need to describe this, the most well-known of the British wild flowers, but perhaps I may reassure you that it grows all over Britain, and prefers light soil and an open spot.

Do I really have to say anything about how to grow a daisy? Except make a plea to gardeners to stop digging them up. Here we are growing lovely flowers, admired throughout history (*bellis* means pretty in latin) and we throw them away!

Transplantation is best after the flowers have gone in October, separating up the clump at the same time though this can be done at almost any time.

Seeds (1.5 × 1.0mm, black and hairy) can be sown in boxes or frames in March, in ordinary soil, 1cm deep and transplanted when large enough to be set out, more than 7cm apart. Outdoors sowing is best in May or June in a sunny spot not surrounded by tall plants. To prevent excessive growth do not divide during the growing season because by the following autumn there will just be many more plants in need of division. The tall plant effect, in which they get light and nutrients robbed from them or frequent moving also have good effects, but as every gardener knows, they are only dealt with ultimately by drastic measures. Fertilisation of their soil gives them bigger, showier flowers, which if removed will stimulate the production of more.

Common Meadow Rue. Greater Meadow Rue. *Thalictrum flavum.*

Perennial. Ordinary soil, slightly acid.

What we see as a sort of cloud of yellow flowers at the top of the stem is in fact a cloud of stamens as the petals, of which there are four, small whitish affairs, are lost early after opening. The yellow fibrous roots give off yearly a 60–120cm stem with small pinnate leaves and this in turn gives, around the end of June for about two weeks, the mist of flowers. It is found in damp parts of Eastern England in wet meadows and the borders of streams and it was collected at one time to dye wool yellow and as a treatment for jaundice.

This is by no means the only type of Rue that can be grown easily in a garden; there are the *Thalictra alpina, minus* and *aquilegifolium* that will do quite well also, but I consider the common variety the most advantageous. Plant it deeply in any reasonably ordinary garden soil, preferably slightly acid, in autumn or spring (March is best), in a moist but partially sunny position and from then on forget about it and let it flower as it likes.

Divide roots in autumn or spring (late March this time) and plant the 3–4cm hairy achene seeds in April in pans of the usual soil, thinning them and planting out when 5cm tall where they are to bloom.

Greater Celandine. *Chelidonium majus.*
Perennial. Light soil.

This is no relation of the Lesser Celandine, so familiar in the spring, but it has the same name because this one really *does* come out around the time that the swallows return from their annual holiday – around May. Growing 22–40cm tall it produces masses of puffy-looking, wrinkled leaves all the way up the stem to arrive at the dozen or so 2cm four-petalled yellow flowers. It is found in lowland Great Britain in hedges and wastes especially near houses because it was at one time cultivated for its bright orange, poisonous sap which was used to treat some skin and eye problems. Not a particularly spectacular plant but pretty. It moves fast about the place under ant-power because its seeds are carried by them in return for a tasty titbit on the side of the seed.

Plant it in March or April in a shady place in ordinary soil and at the same time plant seeds, lightly covered out of doors, thinning them later to about 12cm apart.

Yellow-wort. *Blackstonia perfoliata.*
Annual. Chalky soil.

This is a yellow gentian, flowering from June to October (though some people say that it is earlier) as a 10–30cm annual of sand dunes and limestone turf on the Welsh coast, Central and Southern England. The erect greyish green stem carries the pinnate leaves as almost an obstacle it must pass through on its way to the large yellow flowers that form a terminal cluster.

Sow seeds in October, or as soon as they are ripe, out of doors, in well-drained soil, and thin them out to about 20cm after germinating the following year. This is a difficult process but I see no alternative, so perhaps only those gardeners with 'green fingers' should have a go.

Thrift or Sea Pink. *Armeria maritima.*
Perennial, Porous soil.

A common plant of sea coasts of England and Wales it grows very similar to a tuft of grass but with much smaller leaves and throughout the Summer short stems about 15cm long with a little tuft of pink flowers, each about 5mm across at the top. In the depths of the tuft is the stout woody stock that anchors the plant. Featured on the old threepenny piece, it appears that the reason that this is only found on coast and mountain heath is because of its hardiness to adverse conditions but when it tries to compete for good fertile soil it will be beaten back by any mildly spreading plant.

Plant it in April–May or October in light soil that is well drained (in heavy soil break it up with grit and sand) and give it a good sunny location in a rockery or bed. Division of roots is in autumn or spring, and cuttings can be taken in June and rooted in sand for autumn planting.

Seed use is equally easy, sowing being out of doors in sandy loam in spring and lightly covered, but do not expect a large clump to grow at all quickly. Put other plants round the clump that are not amenable to intense competition, such as Wood Anemones and the clump will grow much better for it.

Cat's-foot. Mountain Everlasting. *Antennaria dioica.*
Perennial. Mountain pastures, poor soil.

This used, at one time, to be a very popular garden plant, but it has now fallen into disuse, surprisingly as it is very attractive and very easy to grow. The plant is stoloniferous and creeps fairly rapidly, rooting at the nodes to give the hairy tight-leaved shoots and the small clusters of pink flowers 2–15cm above the earth. The extreme hairyness of the shoots gave the name Cat's-foot and the fact that it can be dried, preserving the original pink (or white or purple) of the flowers conferred the 'everlasting' part of the name.

A very similar place is filled by it, as is Thrift except in that it can be used for extensive ground cover but anyway they have similar cultivation requirements and methods.

Grass of Parnassus. *Parnassia palustris.*
    Perennial. A variety of soils.
From perennial, pointed roots it sends up a single, leaf-clasp flowering scape, which is hairless, about 50cm tall and carries the white-buttercup-like flower at its summit. Five petals spread out in a 20mm cup with numerous glandular infertile stamens and a few fertile ones around a red ovary form the flower, which appears from July to October. Now for the soil: it is found in boggy places in moist peaty soil, in sand dunes, in damp, basic grassland; thus its main requirement is moisture.

Apparently it came from the South and edged northwards through the centuries, until now it is found mainly in the Lake District and the West of Scotland, while it has become extinct in the South possibly because of the decrease in suitable soil due to intensive farming.

The plant appears, medicinally, to have liver-improving qualities.

The name actually comes from the Mount of Parnassus, which is the house of grace and beauty, and this illustrates the 'perfect' form of the stem and honey-scented flowers.

Divide or plant it in March or April in a moist, shady position, where it has few opponents because it is not a terribly vigorous grower and otherwise it may get overwhelmed.

Seeds (1 × 0.5mm ovoid, grey) can be sown in Spring in a pan of sandy peat, about 5mm down and fairly far apart, thinning and planting out as they grow.

Bistort. Snakeweed. *Polygonum bistorta.*
    Perennial. Damp, ordinary soil.
Late May to late June in some mountainous regions sees a rapid pinking of the grass by the sheer profusion of these flowers. It grows 22–50cm tall from stout rhizome with fleshy leaves and flowers in spikes of pink at the head of the smooth triangular stem. There are some strange things about this plant, for example its name, which refers to the rhizome and means twisted twice; its flowers have no petals but only coloured sepals; its use in the treatment of snake-bites and the improvement in fertility it was meant to have. If you want a splendiferous show from your plants then this one is not for you (similarly *Amphibious Bistort*) but if you like the odd, individually pretty flower, then I think Bistort fits your bill.

A rich moist soil is ideal, but really it is not that fussy and any ordinary soil should be all right. A place in sun or partial shade facing south is good and it should be planted there at the same times as its division, October or March/April. Seeds (3 × 2mm brown and ovoid) should be planted in April out of doors about 2cm apart and thinned as necessary thereafter.

It often does not give such good results when brought into the garden as it does in the wild despite picking off the finished flower heads, which tends to improve the blooming and strength of the plant. Don't rule it out though; it has great curiosity value.

Wood Sorrel. *Oxalis acetosella.*

Perennial. Moist humus. pH 4.5.

Growing from horizontal scaly white roots come the very clover-like three-lobed leaves on a looped petiole allowing them to droop down, and the leafless 10–15cm stalked flowers, which are five-petalled, purple-veined and about 1cm across when fully open. In some cases the late May to early July flowers are a nice lilac colour, though this is rather rare, and there are a few foreign species which get out of hand and quickly become weeds. Just in passing it may be interesting to note that it is found, also, in Japan, so the Beech woods that it likes so much all over Britain cannot be its only favourite habitat. The roots are bitter (hence the name *acetosella*) and were eaten with milk or as a sauce, for which the plant was once cultivated.

Plant it out of doors in a cool, sunny position with acid soil, in autumn, but make sure that there is winter protection and good drainage. Propagation by seeds is rarely practised but rather offsets are taken in spring and watered more and more as they grow. There is considerable variation in the advice I have been given about its favourite site, but I would guess that the very low pH is the first requirement and *that* is the reason for its normally woodland habitat, so it should be all right in the open.

WINTERGREENS

All of the Wintergreens are difficult to grow except *Rotundifolia,* to which we should restrict ourselves at this time, despite the fact that they are all very attractive.

Larger Wintergreen. *Pyrola rotundifolia.*

Perennial. Damp, mossy soil, sand!!

Large, rounded, dark green leaves on short stalks radiate out from the base of the 15–30cm flower stalk and the creeping stringy roots. The flowers are white, coming out from early June to late July, exude a Lily-of-the-valley scent though they have no nectar, and open much wider than those of the smaller flowered, other Wintergreens.

Normally it is found in woodland or damp ground, but with a little ecological cunning, it will grow in a garden. Despite its reputation for being a stubborn plant to raise, it is in fact fairly easy but demanding. Planting should be done in March or April in 45cm of good rich woodland soil (it must be lime free though) in a partially shaded position and spaced about 15cm from its neighbour. Lift and divide it only when overcrowding sets in because it does not like having its roots disturbed and this may be the reason that a plant does not take to the ground well in the first place. The division should be in April, as soon as growth has started. Seed can be sown as soon as it is ripe, in sandy peat, where it is to flower the following year, about 5mm down and well spaced from competition. This method will remove the need for frequent transplantation which, as I said, sets it back for a while.

Larger Wintergreen is rare, so please do not get your specimens by digging them up and transplanting, a process very often unsuccessful, but rather get seeds or consult your nurseryman about it.

Chicory. *Cichorium intybus.*

Perennial. Well drained, preferably calcareous soil.

Yes, this is the famous chicory of the coffee – the root being dried, ground and added to the ground beans, and also the chickory of salads – the young, irregularly shaped leaves being used. From a milky, long tap root grows a very tough, hairy stem often over 60cm tall, and headed by a series of multi-petalled (3–4cm) blue flowers very reminiscent of Hawkbit. Each petal is followed out by a long blue stamen and the whole process of flowering goes on mid-July to early September, opening and closing with the sun. When I said the flowers were blue I should have said that they ought to be blue – if they are red, then it is planted on an ant hill. Normally, however, they are found on roadsides and wastes especially on chalk, becoming more and more common towards the South East of England.

Again there is very little information to be had about its culture but I suppose that the 3 × 1mm achenes could be planted soon after collection where it is to flower – a sunny spot – the following year. It is not all that spectacular, only a few flowers being out at any one moment but the flowering period is very long and it is very attractive though every time I see it I'm sure that a new, blue Hawkbit has just been discovered.

Common Milkwort. *Polygala vulgaris.*
    Perennial. Chalky soils, well drained.
We seem to have a rather boring name for this, a most important ritual plant on the Continent. It is carried in the procession – Rogation day – when the crops are blessed, and gets the name Procession Flower from that. Here, of course, we have the excuse that it flowers too late (late May–early August) for any procession, but we did once find a use for it as a protector of the hermit's house by being planted around it. The plant is a very slight affair with a decumbent stem, vertical flowering shoots usually not much more than 10cm tall and short evergreen leaves, the stem growing from a rosette of them. It is extremely easy to overlook the small spike of pink, blue or white, small (0.5cm) almost bud-like flowers because they are not particularly showy. All over Great Britain it can be found in well drained, preferably calcereous grassland often as a spreading layer but it is not particularly prominent.

Transplant any time that growth is still continuing, though March and April are preferable. Seeds (3 × 1mm) are not easy to get hold of though I suppose that a pan of light soil would take them in March to produce quite rapidly growing seedlings that should be given a place out of doors in a sunny, well-drained spot as soon as they are big enough. The easy method of propagation though must be the division of the plant into rooted side shoots and planting them separately or taking cuttings in summer. I think of the Polygalas as generally trouble free, non-aggressive, slightly vulnerable plants (to grass infiltration) that can be used to fill vacant spots before weeds get there, and perhaps even as lawn-like ground cover because of their evergreen nature.

There are many rare Milkworts which have similar properties but I feel that the common one is good enough.

CHRYSANTHEMUMS

I will deal with the cultivation of wild Chrysanthemums under the well known Feverfew. The ones detailed here are not the prize-winning 15cm flowered varieties but rather the common flowers that were the starting point to so much of that breeding.

Corn Marigold. Yellow Ox-eye Daisy. *Chrysanthemum segetum.*
  Annual. Acid sandy soil.
This is a Swedish export that we are lucky enough to have here scattered particularly around our coastal areas. Growing from both creeping roots and tapering small ones, there is a 15–45cm branched thin, ribbed stem set about by the small, light, toothed leaves. The flowers are in sight from June to September, are 60–70mm in diameter and only slightly scented. At one time it was thought enough of a pest to be worth bringing in a law to eradicate the plant because of the way it overtook crops, but at that point it was discovered that it could be easily controlled by liming, as it can in the garden, because of its abhorrence of non-acid soil.

Ox-eye Daisy or Marguerite. *Chrysanthemum leucanthemum.*
  Perennial. Any soil.
Of course everyone is familiar with this as it is common all over the British Isles and lives happily in the public view at the edges of roads and in meadows. It grows from creeping rootstock to throw up the branching, toothed-leaf plant 23–28cm tall, with a number of the splendid white ray and yellow disc floreted flowers that spread their 5cm from early June to late July and smell rather acrid. Historically they were used for the treatment of asthma, ulcers, and were supposed to keep lightning from striking.

Feverfew. *Chrysanthemum parthenium.*
  Perennial. Most soil.
A branching stem less than 60cm in height gives as it divides the fernlike leaves, and at its tips the round, white and yellow miniature daisy flowers with the edges of the ray florets curled backwards, so characteristic of the plant. It can be seen flowering all over Britain from July to September or even November, always giving its sweet scent. An oil can be made by distillation, which has a very agreeable odour, and this is true of the double variety also.

  It must be remembered that each of the three chrysanthemums I have detailed here has slightly different likes and needs so you will have to vary the cultivation plan to suit them. There are many species derived from *Chrysanthemum indicum × Chrysanthemum morifolium,* which need different methods. Plant in autumn, in well-drained soil, a slightly protected position and away from competitive plants like Bindweed or Mint.

  Seeds (2.0 × 0.7mm) can either be sown directly into a border of moist soil in April and thinned to about 12cm apart or they can be put in boxes and planted out when 5–7cm tall.

Tansy (a chrysanthemum). *Tanacetum vulgare.*
  Perennial. Any light soil.
A clump-grower with feathery leaves coming off the ribbed stem at regular intervals, leaves and branches giving off a lemony scent from the glands.

  The ray florets are missing from the flowers so they just bloom without them in July, August and September as a cluster of 5mm disc floret flowers 30–90cm above the soil. It did have, once, its medicinal uses, a place in the kitchen and as a tonic but its main use was in the oil of Tansy pest repellent, which employed the strong smell. It is common throughout the British Isles.

  Plant it out between October and March in ordinary well-drained soil, with a good view of the sun. Divide the creeping rhizome or roots in autumn or spring, replanting immediately. Possibly invasive, it does not need massive measures to keep it in check, just a good strong wall of daisies or the like will do.

Seeds can be sown in the open in spring and will grow quite happily without protection.

Field Scabious. *Knautia arvensis.*
Perennial. Dryish soil.
Or Biennial.
Long, searching, strong roots, a 90cm stem that is headed by a number of flowers or buds, odd shaped skeletonized leaves, large 4cm mauve flowers, divided up into disc and ray florets and backed by long green sepals, and a flowering period of mid-July to mid-September make up the vital statistics of the plant.

It is found all over the British Isles especially on calcarous soil in hedge-rows, dryish fields and in areas of high drainage that others cannot stand. The name scabious comes from its use as a treatment for scabies though it was also thought to have been used in controlling plague. It produces nectar and has a delicious perfumed honey. Despite having a different genus it can be cultivated like the Small Scabious, but will stand a much greater range of soil. It would look pretty good if it was given a place in a sunny, dryish corner of the garden where it can grow unmolested by weeds because it does not have the foliage to deal with them. Perhaps some Herb Robert round its base could see those weeds off.

Small scabious. *Scabiosa columbaria.*
Perennial. Chalky soil.
What attracts me to the idea that this could be grown in the garden is the fact that its flower head is very similar to that of Field Scabious and fairly large in relation to the rest of the plant and it is easy to contain because it does not creep around very fast and take over the garden; seeds being dispersed by wind. It has fine leaves, a fine 30cm stem, a flowering period from early July to early September and is found in the chalky meadows of Southern, Eastern and Northern England.

With roots, tough and strong, going down 60cm in search of water it has been adapted to living a moist life in a dry place and this is the point to play on if it is to be ridded of competitors. Very well drained soil of loamy sand or chalk (they die off in winter if put in heavy soil) will receive them well if they are planted about 45cm apart in small groups in spring. If the flowers are removed as they fade then, like the seagull laying more eggs until it gets enough hatched, it will put out more. Every 3 or 4 years divide clumps into groups of 2–3 short pieces and replant (after the flowers have gone).

Sheep's-bit Scabious. *Jasione montana.*
Biennial. Non-calcareous soil.
This has an incredibly wide distribution being found right the way throughout Siberia, Northern Africa and the Near East, so this plant is certainly not threatened with extinction. Heaths, mountains, seaside areas, and dryish meadows of the western districts of the British Isles have it in quite an abundance but it is absent from many calcareous soil. The flower heads, at the top of the foliated 7–30cm flowering scape are about 2cm in diameter with very fine, finely made and densely packed florets.

The lower leaves wither while the plant is flowering (mid-May–early September) with its bluey-white flowers, which, though Scabious in form, are not related to the Scabious. It is easily grown where the soil is not too stiff and not chalky, taking easily when planted in either October or March in light, well drained, sandy, loamy soil in a sunny site. Not much more than an annual usually I would suggest sowing seeds in a nursury bed in June and July and then transplanting them to where they are to bloom either that autumn or the following spring. If you want it flowering in the first year then sow the small, oval brown seeds under glass in March or April and transplant to a good sunny place to bloom in late summer (it may need thinning out to a spacing of 10–12cm if transplantation is left fairly late). The extreme success of the plant in colonizing large chunks of the globe show how easily it can enter the garden.

Devil's-bit Scabious. *Succisa pratensis.*
Perennial. Damp land.

A short rootstock (bitten off by the Devil so the legend goes) sends up a very hairy, bristly even, 60cm stem, which is clothed in the hairy rounded leaves and headed by a ball of pretty, mauve flowers which allow their obvious anthers to hang out in the flowering period of mid-June to early October. It appears to be pretty hardy too as it can put up with damp meadows all over Britain except in the extreme North of Scotland. The 2cm diameter flowers attract many insects to their nectar and the leaves can be dried and used for a dye.

As for the cultivation it should be considered like the field and small Scabious because it is a perennial and of a similar nature to them. The points where it strays from this include the habitat which should be damp and can be cold in the winter because it is so hardy. Achenes are about 5mm long and should be planted like seeds, which can be obtained either directly from a wild plant or by allowing the commercial breeds to revert to this form and collecting their seeds then.

Fragrant Agrimony. *Agrimonia odorata.*
Perennial. Acid soils.

Not to put too fine point on it, the difference between this and the next species is that this one has an appreciable smell from the leaves, though not one which could be called perfectly fragrant; a little like turpentine but not objectionable. It grows stout and dark green, a branched stem 60–90cm tall with paler larger flowers than eupatoria, coming out all summer. Uncommon in the South, its grows in acid, shaded soils and it will not stand lime!

Plant in spring in the soil described above, divide the roots at the same time.

Agrimony. *Agrimonia eupatoria.*
Perennial. Any soil.

A cold cure in lemonade, leaves and roots for kidney troubles, dysentery, liver ailments and fevers; the history of its medicinal uses goes back hundreds of years. Growing as a long yellow spike of flowers 30–60cm tall in grassy places, banks and pastures. The leaves vary in size but are all pinnate with the larger ones deeply serrated, the flowers are 6–8mm across but make a good show all together. The roots are woody giving rise to the stiff hairy stem. Between June and August, the flowering period of the plant, they give off a slight scent of ripe apricots but it is not strong enough

to produce an appreciable smell from a distance. It is fairly common all over Great Britain.

The culture of this plant would be similar to that of *Agrimonia odorata* except that it is much less soil selective.

Borage. *Borago officinalis*.

Annual/Biennial. Waste ground.

'I Borage bring always courage' was a saying which is connected with the supposed effect when eaten in salads, the tops being the best part. It was one of the four cordial flowers – borage, alkanet, rose and violet – that made up the ritual drink that exhilarated the spirits. From the stout, flesh coloured, mucilaginous roots comes a rough 24–30cm stem clothed with broad, cubumbery-smelling leaves and headed by a series of 3cm diameter blue five-petalled flowers. These remind me rather of tomato or potato flowers with the spike of anthers from the centre, but they are blue instead of yellow. Originally it was a garden flower but went out of fashion and escaped into the wilds, so now it is distributed in the denser populated country areas on waste, rough ground. There are different types – the annuals and biennials – though both, in other respects, are very similar.

Plant seeds (6 × 4mm black) in autumn or spring annually, where it is to bloom, lightly covered by the ordinary soil and thin, in spring, to 25cm apart. If planting is done in autumn then flowering will be in the following mid-May to late July. It is not particularly showy but will make interesting blooms, and of course there are the herbal properties.

Bugle. *Ajuga reptans*.

Perennial. Ordinary soil.

Found on waste land and damp ground all over Britain, this was once a common garden plant but it fell out of favour because of the ease by which it spread and the difficulty of removing it once it was established. Don't let that put you off, however, because with a good choice of site these things can be controlled. A low spreading creeper, it sends up attractive spikes of blue flowers on a hairy, leafy stem and about 15cm tall. Early May to late June sees the best of the flowers, which though usually blue may be white, pink or almost any shade in between, (blue is certainly the most likely colour). They are 1cm across and are of the upperlipless dragon configuration, having a slight smell and are attractive to bees. Internal wounds were supposed to be susceptible to the healing powers of this plant.

Plant it almost anywhere in autumn or spring and in a position that its ground covering abilities can be put to the best use, round tree bases or rockery edges. The roots can be divided at the same time, just snipping the root connection between plants forming a very quick method to multiply the stock. Seeds can be sown out of doors in any ordinary soil in April, thinning to about 10cm apart. This brings us to the question of how to *stop* the Bugle from covering all the ground. Mowing of lawns in to which it has crept will be a good discouragement, hemming it in by stones in the rockery and planting a wall of things like Willowherb or Dandelions should prevent spread as well, but if in doubt about method then *don't* let it get a hold at all and treat it like Mint.

Comfrey, Coffee Flowers, Abraham Isaac and Jacob. *Symphytum officinale*.

Perennial. A woody herb. Any damp and moisture retentive soil.

This has garden types and most people will have seen it already but maybe know it under one of the nurseryman's names. It is rough so those that are easily allergic to plants better stay away from it for fear of rashes. Grows in leaps and bounds from a tuberous root to produce 30–120cm of hairy and deep green, all-encompassing foliage, with huge leaves culminating with the terminal inflorescence at the tip of the shoot. The flowers, which appear in May and June, are small tubular affairs which curl over like a set of bells and come into bloom one after another gradually changing their colour in the process to become anything from pure white through pinks to deep blue. This plant was at one time cultivated in herb gardens for its leaves from which a tea was made, the roots which gave poultices for sores and bruises and its nuts (6 × 3.5mm black) which gave a blood tonic. It is found throughout Britain and prefers damp shady places.

It will sweep out of the way anything that is occupying possible growing space by its sheer volume of foliage and persistent strong growth, so one needs to know how to retard its growth. Cut it down to ground level in July every three years and that autumn divide the roots, to decrease them to bearable proportions. In a way we should be glad that it grows so fast because of its nice flowers.

Ordinary soil or, if anything special, leaf mould in a shady place in a fairly warm part of the garden suits it the best, being planted there in either spring or autumn. Seeds may take a long time to flower but they can be planted in boxes once ripe and planted out in spring once large enough. Roots can be divided in autumn and this is the best propagating method, though watch out this may not work when the rootstock is infected by the fungus *Melapsorella symphyti* which is specific to Comfrey.

Viper's Bugloss. *Echium vulgare.*
    Biennial usually, sometimes perennial. Well drained soil.
The name Bugloss comes from the Greek for ox-tongued, describing just how rough and hairy the whole plant is. Each of the bristles is so tough that bees often get their wings ripped on them and they will readily bring someone who is allergic to many things out in a rash. The Viper part of the name gives away the use to which the Iberians put the powdered plant – the treatment of viper bites or rabies.

It is a stout erect plant 26–60cm tall, growing from a sort of rosette of leaves and giving off notched pointed leaves on its way up to a terminal raceme of flower sprays. In the axil of tip leaves grows a short curved multi-budded plume of flowers, the ones nearest the stem coming into bloom earliest. Each individual bloom is a short trumpet shaped affair 1.5cm across with many stamens appearing from the depths. They may be any shade from white, through pink (the usual colour of the flower buds) to the usual blue and the shade of the entire plant changes slightly according to this colour. Late May to mid-September sees it in flower on wastes of sandy or gravelly soil on coastal areas generally or inland in the southern half of the island.

Sow seeds (4 × 3mm nutlets) where they are to grow in either the April or August following seed collection, thinning as necessary until they are about 20cm apart. Transplant the following autumn to the position of flowering the following year. This plant makes a fascinating addition to the garden, it is easy, undemanding, not dangerous to other plants or particularly invasive.

Corn Cockle. *Agrostemma githago.*
    Annual. Selective soils.

Back in the early nineteenth century this was incredibly common, known to everyone as a weed but now it is rare and scattered around the country pretty thinly. Even 30 years ago one could see it in profusion, standing about 5cm above the level of the crop and showing off its 2cm diameter lilac flowers all summer. The stem and leaves are hairless and elongated and the flower has five petals, which may at odd times be white. It appears that the reason behind the demise of the Corn Cockle as a common flower has been its poisonous seeds and the effect that they had on the taste and colour of bread! Modern farming methods have produced very pure seeds, which mean that the Corn Cockle does not get itself planted with the crop any more.

In culture it gets the standard hardy annual treatment; plant the black 3mm seeds in early spring where they are to flower, in light moisture-retentive soil and in a sunny situation, thinning out to about 15cm apart. In a way it needs the presence of a wind break as it had in the corn and it almost needs that corn to look right. Somehow it looks so strange alone. Without other plants it will not grow as tall as it usually does, but may give better flowers for it.

THE BEDSTRAWS (*GALIUM*)

Yellow or Ladies Bedstraw. *Galium verum.*
  Perennial. Dryish soil.
A sprawling, common plant of grassy places and banks and meadows, where it straggles over its neighbours. The stem is very fine and very finely divided, again and again until eventually after giving off countless branches and clusters of the needle-shaped leaves, the flowers take over to finish off the stem as a cloud of 3–4mm cross shaped, yellow flowers. From mid-June to early July they give off the scent of fresh hay in their native haunts of coastal, Central and Eastern England. Used in mattresses, used to curdle milk, and the stems made a red dye.
  For cultivation details see Northern Bedstraw (p. 74).

Hedge Bedstraw. *Galium mollugo.*
  Perennial. Dryish soil, preferably basic.
A cloudy affair where the white flowers on a square stem, fit the place where the outside of the cloud would have been, and make the 5–10cm rambling herb look like a patch of mist. Found mainly in shady hedges, open woods and meadows it is a very common plant and spreads out its flowers from the end of May to August. It is particularly common in the South-East and gets gradually less abundant going North.
  For cultivation details see Northern Bedstraw (p. 74).

Crosswort. *Galium cruciata.*
  Perennial. Preferably calcareous soil.
This grows as a cluster of 24–36cm stems growing from a common root-stock and has four-leaved (in the form of a cross) nodes surrounded by a cluster of yellow flowers. Flowers 2.7 × 3mm are around in April and June to give off a sweet, slightly honey-like smell and are divided into male and female types with the male ones lower down than the female.
  It is found on the basic soils of the Midland, the North and Southern Scotland.
  For cultivation details see Northern Bedstraw (p. 74).

Northern Bedstraw. *Galium boreale.*
Perennial. Calcareous rocks.
It grows in the north as an erect plant 15–45cm with creeping roots and slightly larger white flowers and broader leaves than the others I have mentioned, but otherwise very similar.

It flowers in bare, chalky, rocky ground from June to August.

The Galium genus plants should all be given well-drained soil and a sunny position in the open if you want to get the best show from them. I myself find it difficult to collect seeds from them, though from their sheer profusion I would presume that they would produce good plants fairly quickly if planted in light soil in late spring and where they are to flower. Division is a method to which I am much more accustomed and this can be done in autumn or spring leaving a good well-established plant the following summer.

VETCH

And now for a few of the vetch varieties; they're all fairly pretty but only a few can be trusted with a safe place in the garden because either they do not spread very fast or they can easily be dealt with. Believe me, I would like to mention all the plants in this group (like Restharrow, which is rather fine) but some really do creep around too much for my liking so I shall concentrate on the more practical varieties.

Kidney Vetch. Ladies Finger. *Anthyllis vulneraria.*
Perennial. Calcareous soil.
It is found mainly near the sea but will put up with being far from it if given a nice habitat of chalky ground where it may form varieties with deep red to bright yellow flowers on a low spreading plant with small herring-bone-shaped leaves and a long flower stalk. It flowers from May to August and was thought to help wounds heal when rubbed on.

Plant in autumn or spring in poor soil, in a bright spot and add some lime at the same time to improve the leaf colour. Strangely enough the Americans seem to like it for their gardens, whereas in Britain it is considered a weed. Take cuttings of fresh growth in summer, divide in autumn and plant seeds in a frame or sheltered border in April, thinning as necessary to about 22cm apart. Pretty and slightly spreading, it should not provide much of a problem.

Horseshoe Vetch. *Hippocrepis comosa.*
Perennial. Chalky soil.
A chalk or limestone plant flowering, mainly in Central England, from May until July – very much like Birdsfoot Trefoil.

Plant only fairly large plants in an open, sunny spot in summer, in light, preferably chalky soil.

The seed, which should be planted in March in pots of light soil, is slow to germinate and should be kept under glass until the seedlings have grown quite large, when they can be planted out with their potful of soil. Otherwise the horticulture is similar to that of Kidney Vetch (see above).

Tufted Vetch. *Vicia cracca.*
Perennial. Any soil.
A tendrilled climber, with long spiky looking leaves in a sort of herring

bone pattern from the stem. Sprays of pinky flowers are all over the plant, from mid-June to mid-September, as it assaults anything with good tendril holds that happens to be nearby. In fact the relentless climbing is what made it useful to be grown for forage and made it so widespread around Britain. Cultivation is similar to that of the Kidney Vetch (p. 74).

Meadow Vetchling. *Lathyrus pratensis.*
  Perennial. Ordinary soil, sandy.
It was at one time grown as a fodder crop because it did not take much out of the soil being a leguminous plant. The 10mm yellow flowers come in a bunch at the top of a long thin stalk above the coarse, thin, grasslike leaves and winding tendrils that allow it to scale any suitable neighbour. It It flowers from June to the end of August.

  Any soil that is not too extreme will suit it, though it likes a lightish porous soil in which it may be planted in spring or autumn in a sunny place. The existing patch can be split in October but I think that better results are obtained by growing fresh plants from seeds, which are about 2mm in diameter, spherical and dark brown. They should be put 8cm apart and lightly covered by light soil in April and out of doors, where they will grow the fastest if watered thoroughly and kept moist. Something for it to climb on would be a friendly gesture, like a Willowherb plant about 10cm away, and don't worry about weeds, it will probably hold its own.

Bird's Foot Trefoil. *Lotus corniculatus.*
  Perennial. Fairly dry soil.
It grows straggling from decumbent stock to a height of 8–30cm with its clover-like branched stem and leaves, and a clutch of yellow flowers at the top (possibly some double forms as well). The flowers keep coming right the way through the summer from early June to September and it is the way that they are arranged in the shape of a bird's claw that gives the name to the plant. It is found all over Britain and spreads by seeds and underground stems, which are not that troublesome if kept in check.

  If anything is easy to grow, it's this. Cuttings can be taken in summer from fresh growth and rooted in sandy soil to be planted out in autumn. It should be divided and planted in the spring and the seeds, which are 1.5mm in diameter and brown, should be scoured to remove the rough coat, soaked and in April planted 8cm apart out of doors in a well-drained sunny spot.

Melilot. *Melilotus officinalis.*
  Biennial. Chalky soils.
Found on the chalk of South-East and Central England and flowering from June to September, it is a wiry, thinly leaved plant that intertwines on itself with a much-divided stem to finally put up 7cm rods of flowers maybe up to 122cm high.

  Please don't be put off by the spreading nature but rather give it something unstranglable to climb over.

  Golden Melilot and White Melilot are very similar in shape, size and habits to Common Melilot.

  The Melilots are pretty much alike in their garden needs: they are not hardy enough to just be thrown out of the greenhouse too early in spring. Sow seeds under glass in early spring (ordinary soil should do, though make sure it isn't acid) at a temperature of about 60°F let them germinate and then harden them off in a cold frame, taking out all those that look too overcrowded of course. Planting out should be in May or June in a well-drained soil and about 2cm apart. Division or transplanting in spring should be successful and believe me the end product flowers make it all worth-while.

Restharrow. *Ononis repens.*
Perennial. Chalky soil.

I don't suppose that it will surprise you to know that the name 'Restharrow' came about because the plant actually 'arrested the harrow' due to its strong creeping rhizomes. Little shoots come off these at short intervals, giving off small, serrated leaves and, from late June to mid-September, pink, vetch-type, flowers. Usually there are no spines but at times you may run into a plant that has needle sharp points in it. The attraction of it comes not only from the flowers but also from the delicious resinous smell it exudes when bruised, and the edible and tasty roots. Sunny mild localities of chalky or sandy grassland in the heavily tilled parts of England will have an example of it.

This low creeper will take well to light, sandy soil in which it should be potted and planted out. The seed methods of propagation involve growing a small plant in a pot by sowing, under glass, in April and transferring it to its resting position, preferably a sunny spot, in early summer. By far the quickest way to increase the population of your garden is simply by dividing the rhizome into rooted pieces and allowing each part to grow separately. This can be done at any time after the flowers have gone.

RANUNCULACEAE.
BUTTERCUP FAMILY

Lesser Celandine. *Ranunculus ficaria.*
Perennial. Tuberous. Humus rich soil.

The name celandine is supposed to come from the word cheldion, which means swallow, because they were thought to flower around the time that the swallows arrived home from the South. This seems rather strange, however, because they flower mid-March to early May and the swallows are a bit late for that. This is a succulent perennial growing from a sort of claw-shaped set of tubers to produce playing-card-spade shaped leaves and its starry flowers on separate stems. These 'stars' are of shiny buttercup yellow with a diverse number of petals from about seven upwards and a circular centre of short yellow stamens (the whole thing being about 2cm across). I do not think that spring could ever be the same without them and they provide commonly one of the few promises that summer really *will* come despite all the gloomy weather. Medicinally the Celandine gave a cure for 'the King's evil'.

The culture can be divided from the rest of the *Ranunculus* group so I shall deal with it separately. Plant from early autumn to spring, before growth restarts, in humus, rich moisture retentive soil in a position of shade after the leaves have appeared on the trees but in sun up till then. This is not to say, of course, that they will not grow in sun but rather that they hold their own against invading weeds if kept this way. Division of the roots is easy and August and September are the best times for it.

Sow the seeds in moist, humusy loam in spring and plant out as soon as they are large enough to handle into the places that they are to bloom the following spring.

If the thought of the Buttercup as a weed can be put out of your mind for a few moments it should be possible to see that the bloom itself is extremely attractive and, with correct encouragement the plant can produce a glorious show. The following list covers a number of the Ranunculaceae which have varying habitats, so I hope that everyone reading this has at least one plant that his garden will suit. The culture methods are detailed at the end.

Goldilocks. *Ranunculus auricomus.*
Perennial. Any soil

The woodland Buttercup is a small plant, usually less than 30cm tall that grows in hedge banks, shady places and, not surprisingly, woodland. It has rather dainty, three-lobed, skeletoned leaves appearing up the slender stem, which is capped at the top by a few of the buttercup-like and often rather battered flowers. These may have up to seven petals, come out about the end of April, produce small brown achenes and would be better described as a butterplate because they are flatter than the usual. It is found in generally rich soil throughout South-East and Central England, commonly and scattered throughout the rest of the island as well.

Lesser Spearwort. *Ranunculus flammula.*
Perennial. Damp, possibly acidic soil.

A straggling erect plant with creeping stems (40cm), rooting bases, long narrow rather grassy-looking leaves and a bunch of green-centred, buttercup flowers held above the rest on short stems. This is more common in the wetter parts of northern Britain.

Greater Spearwort. *Ranunculus lingua.*
Perennial. Basic, marshy soil.

Very much like the lesser type except, as one would expect, larger (50–100cm) producing solitary flowers at the same periods (June, July, August) and is very uncommon if widespread. This is one of those plants that is suffering from the drainage of marshy and boggy ground. Its habitat is disappearing fast.

Bulbous Buttercup. Common Buttercup. *Ranunculus bulbosus.*
Perennial. Ordinary, dryish soil.

If you don't know the description of this one already, then there is something wrong – 30cm high with a bunch of flowers growing from its base and one or two long, vertical leaved, flowering stems capped by the scaly, shiny yellow cupped flowers, which may look a little orange at times due to the reflections of the orange pollen on the tightly bunched anthers inside.

Flowers 1–2cm across, achenes 3.5 × 2.7mm and flowering from April to June. Found all over the British Isles these have been around for so long and are so widespread that they must have been attributed with a little medicinal power. They were thought to give the yellow colour to the butter, to be a cure for plague and lunacy, and many more.

Hairy Buttercup. *Ranunculus sardous.*
Annual. Heavy soil.

This has paler flowers and hairer leaves than the others in the group, but is otherwise much the same. Its erect 8–36cm stems are common in bare places, cornfields, but especially the coastal areas of the South-East.

Creeping Buttercup. *Ranunculus repens.*
Perennial. Any soil.
This is a large-leaved, leafy runnered version of the bulbous Buttercup (without a bulbous base) except that it is slightly taller and has rather more flowers from the nodes of the creeping stem. It flowers May–September with its 1–3cm flowers in meadows, hedges, wastes, fields and banks.
Very common everywhere.

Meadow Buttercup. *Ranunculus acris.*
Perennial. Dryish ordinary soil.
The big one that stands head and shoulders above the others with its skeletoned five loded leaves and the tall branched stems headed by clusters (I think 'racemed' would be a bit misleading) of the usual type flowers. It is very common in damp meadows and flowers from May to early August. A double form exists to this (though it does not produce seeds).
Buttercups have been generally thus named since the mid-eighteenth century before which they had a variety of names usually to do with the legend that it was their yellow that made butter yellow. In fact it remained a May Day ritual to rub them on the cow's udders. They all have creeping stock and double-forms of most are rare but possible. The corn buttercups are getting quite rare now, due to the use of the selective weed killers.
Plant at any time between November and February with a good 15cm separation to prevent them fighting amongst themselves for soil nutrition, although this soil should be well drained and fertile – perhaps being fertilised with a good chemical fertiliser beforehand. It should get a good, sunny spot with the earth kept moist and will grow profusely possibly needing division every three or so years (spring or autumn) to keep the clump in order.
Seeds should be sown, where they are intended to flower, in the spring or autumn following their collection. There is no need to worry about cold, heat, enemies or pests because once established they will resist anything.

HOUND'S TONGUES

Hound's Tongue. *Cynoglossum officinale.*
Biennial. Dry, ordinary soil.
This is a tall flower 60–90cm in height surrounded and covered low down by its lanceolate, very hairy fleshy leaves. The normally red but often white flowers are quite like the tubular ones of Comfrey, but a bit starrier and they come off the main stem as many separate racemes at the top, each with only a few flowers. It has fleshy tapering rootstock which is rather firmly embedded and 7mm nutlets which are hooked at each end. The flowers, which usually bloom in May and June, can be found in half the world including Britain, throughout the Lowlands on dry soil, in the edges of woods, dunes and downs by the sea.
Cultivation is dealt with under its blue-flowered relative (below).

Green Hound's Tongue. *Cynoglossum germanicum.*
Biennial. Ordinary soil.
This plant is very much like Hound's-Tongue except that it is generally found in the inland areas of the South-East and it has purple-blue flowers. They have both been around so long that it is no surprise that they have medicinal uses, particularly as a narcotic and as a skin disease treatment.

Of course being biennials a new set of plants must be grown from seed every year. Sow the seeds in shallow drills about 15cm apart where the plants are to bloom the following year, or just fairly thinly in ordinary soil in May, June or July to transplant in autumn. The eventual position should be in full sun or slight shade though wherever it is they will fight off many weeds.

Yarrow. *Achillea millefolium.*
Perennial. Ordinary soil.

A tough lad this one, with its dryish, strong roots and a ribbed stem. From the feathery-leaved base the stem leads up vertically some 22–38cm to a plateau of white, 2mm across flowers, which flower from June to October and produce a strong and pleasant scent. It is found on grassland, roadside and wasteland all over Britain, though it may sometimes be in a purple tinged form. The marvellous name *Achillea* comes from its medicinal properties being likened to Styx water, a treatment for bleeding, for colds, as a tonic and as a personality elevator.

The culture method is similar to that of Sneezewort (below), except that it likes life to be much dryer and can hold its own against the majority of weeds, to form a compact attractive clump with broad flowering heads.

Sneezewort. *Achillea ptarmica.*
Perennial. Moist ground.

This is a much slighter plant than Yarrow, to which it is related, thought it is similar in many ways. Flowering from early July to mid-September, it produces the same type of flowers as Yarrow except in that they are much broader with a corresponding increase in the number of petals. This really quite attractive, daisy-like plant was once ground up for its medicinal purposes against toothache (taken like snuff) and for a flavouring with a sharp bitter taste.

It is found all over the country except in some parts of South-East England, inhabiting damp places, ditches, low-lying meadows, hilly pastures, river banks and the like.

Quickly spreading it can be planted in autumn or spring in a sunny spot with moist ordinary soil preferably slightly limey although acidity is not all that much of a drawback. Division can take place at the same time by simply splitting it up into countless rooted fragments that should all take quite well, and I would recommend doing this every three to four years if just to keep the clump in order.

Sow the grey 2 × 1mm achenes in early summer in ordinary soil, 5mm deep, where they are to flower and separate the seedlings as necessary to about 15cm distance from each other. There is a crafty method to store the flowers (it works especially well on Yarrow); in allum. The petals and buds dry out quickly and remain on the stem, giving pretty, long-lasting indoor flowers.

Common Fleabane. *Pulicaria dysenterica.*
Perennial. Any soil.

Traditionally used to alleviate flea-bites, this plant is really easy to grow and keep in place because it does not spread as quickly as it might, even though it has creeping stems. The roots are not pernicious, and they lead to the thick downy stem with its pointed leaves that start from the stem by clasping it. The flowers, from July to September, are in a sort of terminal cluster

that makes the whole of the top of the plant look a golden yellow from the amassed 2cm short-rayed blooms.

It is found in wet places throughout the British Isles and much of Europe.

A very easy plant to grow, it can be planted in autumn or spring in any reasonable soil in a sunny spot and divided into many separately rooted parts in the autumn.

Common Ragwort. *Senecio jacobaea*.
Biennial or perennial. Poor soil.

This plant was supposed to be used by the fairies for travelling in the same way as a broomstick was used by witches. Growing from thickish fibrous roots is the widely branched slightly hairy stem bearing the pointed deeply notched leaves and up to (though more usually 15–75cm) 130cm up a barrage of the yellow daisy-like flowers in a dense head. The flowering lasts from June to October in fair profusion, giving off the 1.0 × 0.3mm fairy seeds that float everywhere. Usually you can see some of it in any grass or wasteland because it is so widespread around the country, but don't bruise it because the smell it gives off is fairly obnoxious (hence the regional names like Stinkweed).

Any soil appears to suit it well in the wild, where it seems to be found in open sunny places, so I would recommend planting in March–April in a warm position.

Seeds should be sown as soon as they are ripe, where the plants are to flower the following year.

How can one get rid of it before it becomes a problem? Cutting it down for two years in succession when it is about to flower will stop it from coming and removal of sprays of flowers before they have a chance to disperse the seeds.

Marsh Ragwort. *Senecio aquaticus*.
Perennial. Damp soil.

Grows 60cm high from the simple roots and has the well-branched stem in common with other ragworts. With its large, pale yellow daisy flowers, it blooms throughout the summer on moist ground throughout Britain.

Its cultivation is similar to that of Common Ragwort except that it should be given a moist, shady position with slightly acid soil.

Pheasant's Eye. *Adonis annua*.
Annual, Chalky ground, mainly.

A feathery, leaved stem leads up its 15–45cm to some pretty, solitary, black-eyed red-petalled flowers, which are about 1cm across and appear from mid-June–mid-July.

The South-East has the greatest concentration of these flowers, but *they are still rare and should on no account be brought back home,* because nature needs help not harm to preserve the stocks.

The flowering period can be increased by the crafty method of sowing two batches of seeds (4.5 × 3.0mm). One in autumn and the other in spring, both in fairly rich soil with good drainage and lightly covered. Do not worry if they take an alarming time to germinate, they always do, and once large enough thin them to about 15cm apart in a sunny spot of similar soil.

Common flax. *Linum usitatissimum*.
Annual. Sandy areas.

Yes, this is the flax used in the production of oil seed, linseed, flax and many of the other by-products that fuelled the industrial revolution. *Linum* comes from the Celtic word meaning 'a thread' so you can see just how long it has been used to make cloth. The places in which it is now found in Britain are those where it was once cultivated, i.e. the Lowlands. It has gone out of agriculture now because of the way that the many crops per year would take such goodness out of the soil, and mean a long time for recovery of the land. You will not be surprised to hear that it is a straggling plant with fine stems and fine leaves but from late June to mid-July, at least, it has lovely bright blue five-petalled flowers that are about 15mm across and very attractive. We now have special garden varieties of linum, but it is worth growing this, if only as a tribute to its incredible history that took it all over North America, Europe, Asia and now Australia as a productive crop.

Of course the way to grow this is from seeds, sown in a cold frame in early March in ordinary light soil, shallowly and thinned as necessary. Later in spring, the 5 × 3mm flattened, brown seeds can be planted outside, where it is to bloom, and thinned until the seedlings are about 12cm apart. Give it a sunny place and pull out the whole intertwining mass once the flowers have gone, to minimize the number of seeds that are self sown.

Greater Stitchwort. *Stellaria holostea.*
Perennial. Herbaceous. Any soil.

Maybe I'm the only one who likes this as a garden plant, but I still maintain it has its uses and will help to protect any bare ground from invading weeds. The hairless, (square in cross section) stem grows from fibrous looking roots, which will spring from many parts of the stem and allow it to creep, carries along its 60cm numerous, hairless, grassy looking leaves, and at its tip plenty of white, starry flowers. Five petals, divided into two halves by an indentation, form a background for the many stamens with their obvious yellow anthers which hang in front, constitute the pretty 2cm flowers in the months from April to June. This rambler is easily removed just by pulling and will die back quickly if replacement shoots are pulled out too.

It likes damp, shady places, hedgerows, woodland margins and of course, similar places within the garden where it is useful to keep the weeds down.

Sea Aster. *Aster tripolium.*
Perennial. Salty ground.

Long tough fibrous roots give off a 90cm stem with leaves coming off singly up to the head of purple outer floreted/yellow inner floreted daisy-like flowers which are about 2cm across and appear from early August to late September. The flower spray is large and this attracted the Elizabethans to grow it in their gardens, where it was cultivated in masses to give the best, 'blaze of colour' effect. The rhizomous stock was at one time used as a wound herb. It is found all over Britain in muddy, sandy and rocky coastal areas and in salt marshes inland.

The roots of the plant can be affected by wilt; when this is the case the ground should be rested for four years before replanting.

Plant it, massed for best results, in spring in any damp salty ground (add crushed rock salt every so often), in a sunny position. Division of the crowns can take place at any time during spring up until June and in summer cuttings of flowerless new growth can be rooted in moist sand for autumn planting outside. Seeds should be sown in autumn and *thickly* where they are to bloom the following year, thinning out those that germinate to about 20cm apart. The reason that I stressed that large numbers of seeds should be sown initially is because there is, for some unknown reason, a very low germination rate. I don't suppose that the intractable weeds will be put off by the salt around but Thrift would certainly deter.

FUMITORY

Yellow Corydalis, Yellow Fumitory. *Corydalis lutea.*
  Perennial. Any soil.
This is another former garden plant that was given up when it became too common in the wild (though a few people still grow it) and a native of Southern Europe, where it lives, as it does here, on walls and among rocks. A fleshy rootstock gives rise to 30cm stems with pinnate leaves in pairs low down and flowering stems opposite leaves further up. The leaves themselves are dainty and fernlike and the yellow, elongated flowers, which all face the same way on the erect flower stalk keep 5–7cm inches above them. They flower in England and especially the South East, from July to September.
  Plant in Autumn or Spring in good sun, a warm spot, and light, well drained soil. Divide the plants up into rooted segments after flowering has finished, and sow the 1.7mm, spherical black seeds thinly in a cold frame of light, sandy soil in April, thinning later to 7cm apart, outside.

White climbing Fumitory. *Corydalis claviculata.*
  Annual. Acid soils.
A delicate and smooth plant climbing 15cm to 2 metres around anything that will support the tendrils it sends out from the end of its petioles. The white (June to September) flowers come in little spikes scattered up and down the plant of 6–8mm individual blooms all facing the same way on the stem. Scattered all over Great Britain fairly thinly, but concentrated by the coast in stony, bushy places and in hilly districts.
  Sow the small black seeds, where they are to bloom that year, in ordinary soil in April, thinning to 20cm apart. They like a sunny spot and will hold their own against, indeed climb up and smother, plants near them, though there is little danger of it becoming a pest. Plant in the same spot the next year (they self sow rather too easily) or weed out in spring and they should prove little trouble.

KNAPWEEDS

And now for a quick swoop through the Knapweeds, which are nice plants but here in Britain, certainly, a large number of them are very similar.

Lesser Knapweed. *Centaurea nigra.*
  Perennial. Ordinary soil.
A very common plant throughout the British Isles, with its hard flower head that gives it the name Hardheads in some parts. The plant is really pretty tough all over with tough stems, tough roots and a very hardy nature,

allowing it to grow in almost any climate as long as there is enough light. Flowers with characteristic Knapweed bloom in a bright pink from late June to early September.

Plant it in November or March, dividing the roots at the same time if the group is over crowding. (Throw away old plants if you can spare them because they will gradually degenerate). It should get basic soil if anything, light, well drained, and a sunny position, spaced about 20cm apart. Seeds (long, thin affairs) should be planted in a frame or out of doors in April or May and then transferred when 2cm tall to a nursery border to be planted in the permanent place the following spring.

The plant from this series that I prefer is the:

Greater Knapweed. *Centaurea scabiosa.*
Perennial. Basic soils.
Larger, showier, brighter flowers with sterile outer florets (as may be the case with Lesser Knapweed) a preference for basic soils in grassland, rough scrub and wasteland, being found in England generally, and flowering early June to late August, separate the two species, but they are similar in many ways. Both of them for instance were used to foretell the future by taking off the unexpanded florets of the flowers and if the other florets open afterwards then the owner will soon fall in love. It is easier to control in colder parts of Britain where the temperature does not allow it to spread too fast; in the South, though there may be a different story.

Cultivation is similar to that of the Lesser Knapweed.

Colt's Foot. *Tussilago farfara.*
Perennial. Small. Clay soil, but any poor soil will do.
The whole plant preserves itself and reproduces by means of the thick and woody rhizome from which the flower stem first appears in the spring (mid-March–late April). It is a scaly green stem about 10cm tall that holds up the dandelion-like one inch flowers; as with dandelion, they seed by the plume seeds 7.0 × 1.2mm. The leaves come after the flowers have come up and they are generally fairly rounded and fleshy. It was grown as a herb until fairly recently, as a cure for a cough (tussis – cough) and for the herbal, tobacco, beer, jelly and wine flavouring properties, most of which used the properties of the rhizome (a succulent thing) and the leaves (especially wine). It is found all over Great Britain and spreads basically by the seed method though it can invade quickly through its roots. Despite this property, it cannot hold its own against many other plants so that it is ousted or at least pushed to one side by anything that takes up sunshine. And note, it should be in a position to reach the winter sun because it is there before the leaves on the trees. It particularly likes clay soil but it is the first to arrive after some marl of limestone rubble is left.

It is easy to cultivate; a piece of the rhizome will shoot in the right season if planted out from October to January so that it can flower that year in its new position. Soil that it is put in can be of any kind, but you should make sure that the Coltsfoot has nothing to fight with. This method is much more reliable than seeding, although the seed produced is prolific due to the very much larger numer of female than male flowers in the floret population. Do not worry about them being in the slight shade once the trees have foliated because they should be over and done with by then. During the rest of the year they can be mutilated in many ways and they will still be back to fight again in the years ahead. It takes hard hoeing and selective weed killers to get rid of them eventually. In other words it is a

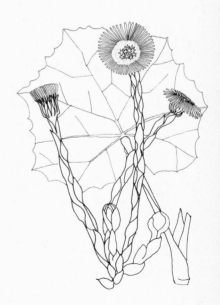

84

good thing to contain them in some way with fast growing and thick flowers so that they are hemmed in.

THISTLES

Spear Thistle. *Cirsium vulgare.*

Being a biennial it should be no surprise to learn that it is not exactly exciting in its first year being a sort of plate-shaped star of the usual thistle with spiky leaves close to the ground. In its second year it forms the tall regal multiflowered specimen we would expect from the plant that is the symbol of Scotland. Large 5cm flowering heads with a purple cluster of petals each adorn the top of the plant found in waste places, scrub land and hedgerows all over Britain from July to October. The leaves are sharp and contorted with hairy undersides.

Easily controlled by mowing down before seeding. Heavy gardening gloves are essential when dealing with any of the thistle family.

For cultivation see under Melancholy Thistle (below).

Scotch Thistle. *Onopordum acanthium.*

Biennial. Any soil.

There is in fact a battle between this and the last species I mentioned as to which has the rightful title of being the Scottish emblem, in fact, the motto 'nemo me impune lacessit' (no one attacks me and gets away with it) should belong to the former species because this, despite its name, is found in parts of East Anglia where it is rare even there. From a rosette of spiky lanceolate leaves, which follow the flowers up the stem grows the tall tough pillar of the plant up to the 7cm diameter head. Other differences from the Spear Thistle are that it has solitary flower heads, and appears to like stream sides particularly.

Put a moist ground tinge on the cultivation method of the Melancholy Thistle to get it growing best.

Melancholy Thistle. *Cirsium heterophyllum.*

Perennial. Damp, ordinary soil.

The reason that I put this into the list is because of its very attractive nature and the fact that it could do with some help in retrieving its former position being now rather rare and almost confined to the mountains of Northern Scotland. It grows from 30cm to 2 metres tall from woody roots, leaving its 5cm flower heads to droop down from the top in some cases.

It blooms from late June to mid-August. Give it a sunny position in well-drained soil by planting 30cm apart in spring or autumn. Seeds should be sown (every year in the case of the biennials) 2cm deep out of doors in April or May and transplanted when 7cm high to their flowering position for the next year, setting them 30cm apart. All of the thistles have a dominating character to the areas of garden around them, providing tall, attractive plants, and defying goodness-grabbers such as privet roots.

Corn Sow Thistle. *Sonchus arvensis.*

Perennial. Waste ground. Any soil.

This tall leafy plant grows up to 90cm from a white subterranean stolon as a thick stem with very hairy, pretty sharp leaves coming off the plant as the stem divides. The 4cm flowers are dandelion-like and come out from July to September as terminal clusters on the hollow, milky juice-containing stems. It is found all over Britain in cornfields, marshes and waste ground.

Thistles proper are splendid, extrovert creatures that will battle against almost anything to show themselves off right where you don't want them. Therefore, in case of dire necessity, there had better be a description of how to get rid of them. From my own experience, pulling out the rosette of leaves at the thistles base, along with its roots should be successful first time but if there is a recurrence then a re-removal will see it off. Pull the flower heads off as they fade as this will take away their legacy of silky pappused air-born seeds.

White Horehound. *Marrubium vulgare.*
Perennial. Prefers chalky soil.
A hairy (hence the word 'hore') plant growing about 30cm tall with its mint or nettle-like stem and leaves, coming from a cluster of woody, rhizomed fibrous roots. The flowers appear as little bunches, small and white in the axils of the upper leaves from the beginning of June to the beginning of October and form rather interesting balls of white, though the plant cannot really be described as being particularly striking. The main use for it, is in its herbal capacity, having a bitter taste, and scented leaves. A tea can be prepared from it, a beer and an extract that was supposed to be good for the treatment of colds. It is also one of the five bitter herbs of the Jewish Passover. I would not have said that this plant is extremely common but it does seem to have a very wide distribution around Britain, mainly on waste ground, commons and roadsides.

Plant seeds out of doors in late spring in well-drained ordinary soil with a little lime added. The 2.5 × 1.5mm nutlet grey seeds should be put 1cm down and about 30cm apart, because they will surely, given a light shady place, produce enough foliage to fill the gaps.

Root cuttings can be taken, and planted in similar soil to that above but in April and planted out once they poke through. It is very hardy.

I told you that it was a spice, well perhaps you would like to make some fudge from it. The process is simple:

Boil leaves together in sufficient quantity to make water taste strongly, and leaving at least ½ pint of liquid. Remove leaves, add 1lb sugar. Bring the mixture to the boil, then lower heat to cook gently. Test by dropping in cold water, if it can be rolled in a soft ball between the fingers, the fudge is ready. Add butter and beat it with a wooden spoon until creamy and beginning to set. Pour into a buttered tin and cut into squares.

Bastard Balm. *Melittis melissophyllum.*
Perennial. Dryish soil.
Extremely suitable for the garden with its large white and pink strongly scented (like sage) flowers in a leafy head to the short (usually less than 30cm) hairy stem, it grows as a tidy, thick bunch, spreading slowly and it's easy to control, despite its creeping roots. It dies down in winter but gets going early enough in spring to produce blooms by May, which, by the way, attract hawk moths, (specially adapted by having a long enough tongue to reach the nectar of which copious amounts are produced).

It grows on woodland margins and dry banks, almost entirely in the warm, wet South-West, though despite this indicator, it is really quite hardy.

A nice place, away from competitors in semi-shade will do fine, though it should have a good rich loam to ensure that it thrives. Divide the rhi-

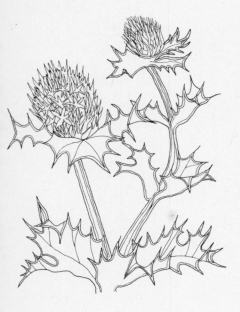

zomes in autumn after the flowers have gone and replant in similar conditions immediately. Seed sown in spring will do well if this is done out of doors and in rich soil. Plant fresh plants any time from October to March.

Sea Holly. *Eryngium maritimum.*
  Perennial. Sandy, gravelly soil.
For even such an odd shaped plant – greyish/green holly leaves, ribbed low (6–18cm) stems with a globule of many small blue flowers on each – it certainly has some strange uses. All over European coasts its young flowering shoots are eaten like asparagus, its parsniplike rhizomatous roots are candied and sold, and it is 'specific for all complaints arising from flatulence' (Dioscorides). The flowers, each five-petalled, 4mm across and blue, form a spiny head 2cm across during July and August, which dries and is maintained later in the year. It can be found generally on sand or shingle on English sea coasts especially towards the west.
  For a plant that was grown in gardens, I can find very little about its cultivation, merely that it likes a well-drained spot in the sun and its seeds should be planted out of doors in April. Divide in March.

Elecampane. *Inula helenium.*
  Perennial. Ordinary soil.
  I put this in, not only because it looks nice, but also because of its widespread medicinal and religious uses, which make it a plant worth discussing. It grows from thick, branching, aromatic tuberous roots, which were used in the distillation of absinthe. It has a number of broad hairy root leaves, which were used to make a tobacco, and a single flowering stem clasped by more of the hairy leaves. Growing up to $1\frac{1}{2}$ metres high it may only produce a few flowers, which are like very broad yellow daisies with thin ray florets. Originally it came from the Caucasus for its supposed healing properties for plague, tuberculosis, bronchitis, it was used as a diuretic and as a general do-good. With this kind of reputation it is not surprising that it has found its way to the USA as well, so it should be said that there must have been something pretty convincing to the people who grew it that it worked. Most of the cures came from the root, which was dried and smelled like violets. Fascinating but not that excitingly beautiful.
  To grow it yourself is simplicity itself, by planting between October and March in a sunny spot and ordinary soil. In the wild it is scattered all over Britain and found in damp places so it is pretty amenable to the cold and wet. Seeds can be sown out of doors in April and June where it is to flower and from then on it can be just left to itself apart from the periodic splitting (in autumn or spring) to ensure that the clump does not spread too far. Put something spreading round its base – Restharrow perhaps – to stop the effects of its seeds, and it should be no trouble.

WILLOWHERBS

Rosebay Willowherb. *Chamaenerion angustifolium.*
  Perennial. Where there has been a fire or really any waste land.
A hundred years ago this was a rare plant in Britain but with help from the stock of the Canadian breeds it was taken up to brighten the gardens of land owners because of its tall, long-lasting plume of pink flowers (which give it the name of Fireweed in some parts of the country). This is a conspicuously tall plant growing from creeping rootstock as a simple flowering

stem with wavy, willow leaf shaped, spirally arranged leaves clothing its lower two-thirds. This makes it a very leafy plant with the leaves clustered along the stem and pointing upwards where they are closely packed and hanging horizontally when the plant has plenty of room. Two centimetre, five petalled, stalked flowers come off the reddened upper part of the stem and they flower in succession starting off with the lowest and gradually working up the raceme, so that at any one time within the late June to September flowering period there are some flowers in every stage of development and some seeding.

Yes, as I'm sure you already know the seed part of this is the insidious part. The outer covering breaks off to reveal a cottony pappus, which spreads out carrying the seeds off in the wind. This is probably the reason that it fell out of favour with the gardeners because although the young shoots are easy to control (and can indeed be eaten like asparagus tips) they have become too common in the wild to warrant being a garden favourite. It has long creeping underground stems which become a nuisance and in winter its leaves die off leaving the woody canes behind.

Again, may I stress that Willowherbs in general grow like wildfire and will not be stopped by much because of the depth of the underground roots. Control, which could be more of a problem than encouragement, can be done by pulling out the newly formed shoots for two years in succession and this will sufficiently discourage the roots to stop them trying again usually. They are a tremendous joy during flowering but afterwards a thick brown stake is left and often a few ragged dead leaves, so their removal when they have threequarters finished their season will tidy up the garden.

Pretty 'fairies' of a pappus-enclosed seed are produced in copious quantity and these might be a delight to watch but they are a sign of quick spreading. This brings me on to their culture. Divide and plant in autumn in any moist, rich soil. Sow seeds where to bloom (slight shade I hope) in autumn or spring.

The only differences relating to Great Hairy Willowherb are that it needs much damper soil and it doesn't present so much of a threat through invasion.

Great Hairy Willowherb. *Epilobium hirsutum.*
Perennial. Moist ground, by pools.
Pretty in its way with masses of foliage and a good healthy growth, this flower has made it up to 4–5 metres in moist conditions (the moister the taller) giving out plenty of paired leaves on its way up. Pink flowers come out in succession at the top of the plant thus giving a modicum of its four-petalled 2cm flowers all summer. Just like the other Willowherbs I have mentioned it is easy to grow and grows very strongly almost getting to any height to reach a good light source. Because of its wide distribution it has attracted many local names through the centuries. If you want to have a go at this and keep it for many years then you should watch that there are others of its species close by, because it must be cross pollinated (its flowers need pollen from other plants to fertilise their seeds) and also watch out because it may spread like 'wild fire'. For culture details see the Rosebay Willowherb (p. 86).

Common Centaury. *Centaurium erythraea.*
Annual. Any dryish soil.
The name Centaury comes from the centaurs of the Greeks because they

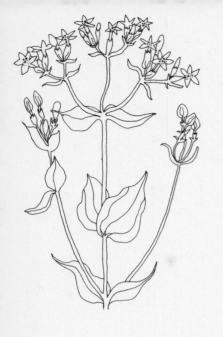

were supposed to have used it as medicine and indeed, for many years the practice continued as a treatment for gout, and liver disease. The tapering fibrous roots sprout a 30cm shoot that bear paired leaves up to a plateau of 1cm pink flowers, the head being about 5cm across and appearing from mid-June to early October. (There is also an albino version). It is found mainly on coastal areas of England and Wales, but it grows inland quite well on dry grassland especially in sandy areas and will form crowds in the right conditions. It is difficult to grow.

The only tip that I can give is to plant the seeds as soon as they are ripe in autumn, light soil and in an open dryish position.

Seaside Centaury. *Centaurium littorale.*
Slender Centaury. *Centaurium pulchellum.*
Dumpy Centaury. *Centaurium capitatum.*
These are very similar in many ways to the Common Centaury but they are much less common. If you would like to cultivate them it should be possible to use the same method as for their common relative (excepting that *Centaurium capitatum* is a perennial) but again their culture is difficult.

Teasel. *Dipsacus fullonum.*
Biennial. Ordinary soil.
Every one must have seen this plant or at least its flowers after it has been allowed to dry out and used as decoration; it looks like a spherical pin cushion on a stick. In life however, the teasel is a tough, thick, sharply stemmed and leaved, very thistle-like plant with a branch stem 1–2 metres tall with a ball-shaped flower (looking just as it did dried but with a green tinge and a layer of purple flowers round the base). It blooms in mid-summer and stays in place all through the winter. The medicinal use of the plant came from the rain water that collected in the 'cups' formed by the way the leaves come off the stem and was thought to cure warts. Real, live teasels will be found in the warmer parts of the country, i.e. coastal areas and South East of a line from the Humber to the Exe estuaries, in roadsides, meadows and wasteland.

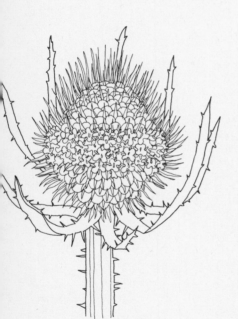

This is one plant to give a place to itself not only because it looks magnificient and stately but also because it will not tolerate much competition within 30cm. Sow the 5.0×2.5mm achenes in well-drained chalky loam in a sunny place in the period April–June and thin the seedlings to about 4cm apart, planting them in their eventual positions, also open and sunny, in early October. If you don't remove the head it will remain on a dry plant all winter shedding a few achenes to self seed and start the next generation. Take the heads off, and leave them to dry so that they will take spray paint and they will make pretty ornaments.

Meadow Goat's-beard. *Tragopogon pratensis.*
Perennial. Open land. Any soil.
This is a native of the temperate regions of the Northern hemisphere in general, so Britain is just one of the many countries to have this sap-rooted, 40–75cm plant with thin grass-like leaves and a clock not unlike that of the dandelion. The narrow leaves chase the flower up the stem by sheathing it up to about 10cm from the flower. One of the old names for this plant was Jack-go-to-bed-at-noon on account of the June and July flowers often closing at around midday. Found in England generally and sheltered coastal waters elsewhere in the British Isles it may have been

deliberately moved by man because its roots were once eaten (tasting like asparagus) before the shoots came up.

Plant in any good garden soil in a half shade or sunny position in spring or autumn. The seed can be sown out of doors in early spring 1cm apart and thinned out later. The beauty of the plant lies to my mind in the fineness of the flower.

HAWKWEEDS

Admittedly I can't see many people rushing out and trying to grow Hawk-weeds – it seems that most gardeners have had a running battle against them for years – so actually inviting them back into the garden would almost be sacrilege.

All I can say to that is there are some types that are not quite as invasion as others and are beautiful as well! Hard to swallow perhaps, but true up to a point: the ones I list here are not as invasive as some, but they still have to be watched.

Smooth Hawk's-beard. *Crepis capillaris.*
  Biennial. Any soil.
The advantage of this smooth (though somewhat hairy) plant is that it has a branched head of flowers, which are each up to 2cm across, coming out from June to October and giving way to a silky pappus when finished. Again this is happy on almost any poor soil where it has room to move with its basal Dandelion-like leaves and some following up the 30cm stem.

Mouse-eared Hawkweed. *Hieracium pilosella.*
  Perennial. Grows on any soil.
On banks, fields, grasslands, wastes, anywhere they will come and take up residence quite quickly and possibly be difficult to eradicate so may I recommend putting them in a spare corner of the garden. This one is rather variable in its height (7–40cm), in its number of flowers, (usually one only) and in the shape of its leaves but usually it keeps itself to itself in one place by having hairy daisy rosettes of leaves with a small dandelion flower, (20mm diameter). It does have creeping runners but they are easily dealt with.

The culture of all of them, despite their separate genuses is similar, though again I refer you to the notes on each one as to the habitat preference. It all follows common sense. Plant in spring or autumn in open places as a transplant and plant seeds in spring out of doors and where they are to flower. If you find that they are not hardy enough as seedlings then do that under glass and transplant to their resting position in June but don't expect a flower the first year despite this easy treatment.

A warning – the hairy pappus on the seeds, which are themselves small and rodshaped, will carry seeds all over the garden and perhaps settle and germinate. I say perhaps because *these* are not as invasive as many others but rake off the flower heads once dead anyway.

Rough Hawkbit. *Leontodon hispidus.*
  Perennial. Chalk and limestone soil.
This is of the clock variety in the way that it holds its pappus when the 2cm diameter flower finishes, being about 24cm up on the flower stalk.

The shoot grows up and flowers from June to late August, a rough and hairy affair.

Orange Hawkweed. *Hieracium aurantiacum.*
  Perennial. Ordinary soil.
Everyone knows the Common Yellow Hawkweeds, which are quite attractive in themselves, without the special colouring of this plant. Orange flowers, about 15mm across in very much the same style as the other Hawkweeds and appearing in June and August. The stem is from 15–75cm long and is clothed in the lanceolate, hairy leaves that also spring from the creeping horizontal rhizomes. It has fallen out of favour as a garden plant (it was originally imported for the garden) and has found its new home on waste ground, all over the country.
  Its cultivation is very similar to that of other Hawkweeds.

Yellow Archangel. *Galebdolon luteum.*
  Perennial. Sandy or heavy soil.
On first sight this looks just like a bright yellow and less leafy version of white Deadnettle, with exactly the same type of flowers and the serrated leaves on a 38cm flowering stem. It is common in southern Britain and rather rare in the North. The May–June flowers have bright red dots on the insides where the teeth of the snapdragon would have been and they die out to leave a 3.5 × 1.5mm tetrahedral nutlet. Long runners of a slightly lighter green also follow the flowers and these allow the plant to spread rather quickly so watch out for them and stop their progress especially in the damp, shady places on heavy soils that it loves so much. Many people tell me that they don't like the smell too much but you have to go out of your way to be able to smell it.
  It should be planted in spring just as the new shoots are a few inches tall and it is then easy to gauge the depth in which it should go in the moist, heavyish soil. Give it a place in the shade where its roots, by which it perennates, don't get dug up. Division of the clump is by splitting up the rooted pieces of the leafy runners and planting them all separately. The nutlets should be planted, for preference, where they are to flower the following year, in a damp shady place as soon as they are ripe. If you develop a passion for this type of flower then there are White Deadnettle, Red Deadnettle, and Yellow Rattle to keep you busy.
  Archangel is not particularly aggressive and should be little problem to control especially if surrounded by evergreens or strong autumn plants.

MINT

There are many marvellous and tasty kinds of Mint in Britain. They are in general not particularly showy but they will easily keep down other less culinary useful plants and provide a sweet scent where one is wanted.
  If you manage not to grow any of these, then I suggest that the soil be tested because, to coin a phrase 'Mint grows everywhere'. You just can't go wrong. In the horticultural boffin's books it gives detailed descriptions of methods, which are not really needed. Transplant small specimens (I say small because it's easier and will grow big) in spring or autumn to a fairly shady place where it can do little damage by spread – perhaps surrounded by brickwork. To propagate just pull up a piece of plant along with a scrap

of root and replant wherever wanted; this ease means that seed is rarely needed in the garden.

Now for the warnings. It will take over if left alone because of the roots that have a tremendous reach underground and will stop at nothing, so hem it in with good strong healthy plants, e.g. Willowherb or Thistles. It fatigues the soil fairly quickly so give it a good feed once in a while of bonemeal and nitrates.

Corn Mint. *Mentha arvensis.*
Perennial. Ordinary soil.

Fast creeping, sweet scented, and about 60cm tall, this is a common plant of waste land and damp woods. It flowers with the usual mint-type purple bunches around the nodes and among the terminal leaves from the end of spring to the beginning of autumn.

Spear Mint. *Mentha spicata.*
Perennial. Ordinary soil.

At one time I used to think that this was purely some kind of chewing gum, such is the effect of advertising, I suppose. Any way the Spear Mint has been grown in gardens for a long time and all I can do is to say what a strong spreader it is, with creeping stems and an ability to grow past almost anything. It is scented and can be seen flowering by streams, in damp places and in roadsides throughout Britain, in August and September.

See above for horticultural comment.

Water Mint. *Mentha aquatica.*
Perennial. Damp soils.

Any damp place, stream banks, ditches, are liable to get some of this because it is very common, having strong hairy stems, a strong scent, and flowering from early August to late September.

This is not quite as invasive as the others, partly because it has to stay near water, but otherwise its propagation is the same and detailed above.

Dandelion. *Taraxacum officinale.*
Perennial. Any soil.

Well if you do not know this one by now you must have a very overworked gardener because it grows everywhere on almost any soil and spreads rapidly. Growing from a long tap root there is a turf of long, deeply serrated pointed leaves and a single hollow, juicy, stem crowned at the top of it with a yellow composite flower 15–35mm in diameter flowering from March to October and giving small achenes on a hairy papus. Do not think that it's always been a weed please, because it has been harvested by many races as a source of herbs. For example as a replacement for chickory in coffee, the root essence has been used and the leaves have been used as salad. Wine has been made as well as jellies and diuretics! but the only thing that has remained elusive is a flower that does not close up when picked.

There are two species of *Taraxacum* that differ from the Common Dandelion very slightly, the main mark of distinction being their love of wet places; they are *Taraxacum palindosum* and *Taraxacum spetabile*. If any one does want to encourage the Dandelion then, not surprisingly the way is very clear.

Transplant autumn or spring, lift and store roots in November, sow seed out of doors in infertile soil (this gives it a headstart against others which need good soil) and thin to about 20cm apart. Feeding with nitrate fertiliser once they are fairly large will increase the size of the bloom enormously.

Take seeds from the dead head. To make the leaves suitable for eating, they must be blanched by putting them in the dark or tying them, still on the roots, in bundles around the flower stem so that only the outer ones receive light.

THE CLOVERS

One of the products of modern agricultural methods has been the production of huge polyploid (species in which the chromosome number of the plant has been multiplied) versions of clover and their use in the growth of fodder. The natural clovers are nowhere near as spectacular as these giant versions and even they cannot be said to be ablaze with colour. This is not to say that it is impossible to grow very flowery versions because certain strains have been produced horticulturally for this purpose and they are pretty good. If you want a four leaved clover lawn it can be done by transplanting a congenitally four-leaved plant and allowing it to spread, but this takes time and it should be noted that in the wild the seeds are not true to this four (or even five) leaved character and the offspring usually revert to earlier type.

There is one very good reason to go for the wild clovers – their lovely scent (mainly in white clover) which is sweet from the copious volumes of nectar that is produced.

CRUCIFERAE. CABBAGE FAMILY

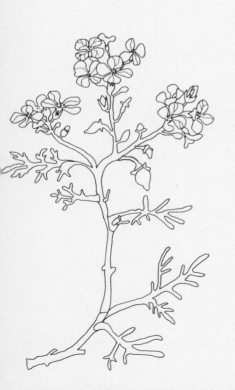

Woad. *Isatis tinctoria.*
Biennial. Sandy or gravelly soil.
This is really a native of Assyria imported here many hundreds of years ago to be used in the production of dye, which, until about the mid 1930s, still actually went on around Glastonbury ('glas' means blue and it was the dye that gave it the name) though it was a tedious process. The seeds were sown between May–June on open ground and may have given as many as three or four crops a year, exhausting the soil but providing the seed pods for the factory. It is found in dry and stony places on gravelly soil, particularly around the valley or the River Severn. Being a pointed leafed, 35–70cm tall crucifer with a raceme of yellow small flowers, it is not particularly striking but it has oddity value.

The list of flowers in the Cruciferae family is long, and I could go on telling you all about how to grow these tall plants all night, so I had better say that some are not all that rewarding and tend to get a good hold of any unsuspecting garden. Just a list I think will do, but please don't write off all the species here because it is always a delight to deliberately grow a wild flower if only just to find out that it is always much nicer than expected.

The flower is likely to self pollinate, this being most likely in wet weather.

Wallrocket. *Diplotaxis tenuifolia.*
Stinkweed. *Diplotaxis muralis.*
Hedge Mustard. *Sisymbrium officinale.*

Treacle Mustard. *Erysimum chieranthoides.*
Charlock. *Sinapsis arvensis.*
Field Cabbage. *Brassica campestris.*
White Mustard. *Sinapis alba.*
Black Mustard. *Brassica nigra.*
Field Pennycress. *Thalaspi arvense.*

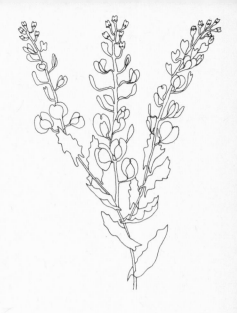

Turkscap Lily. *Lilium martagon.*
    Perennial. Rich soil.
Despite what some people may have said about it being introduced recently
from the Far East (it is a native of the mountains of Greece, Central Europe
and Russia) it has been around much longer than that, possibly since the
time of the Crusaders and this is corroborated by the fact that it is con-
spicuous by its absence from Ireland. It grows from a spear-shaped yellow
bulb that may be cultivated for its taste; like that of a potato. The stem is
60–90cm tall holding the fusiform leaves and many flowers, which appear
in August and September and are typically lily-shaped, with a set of red
petals dotted on the inside, and a prominent set of stamens. The heavy
perfume that it makes attracts the butterflies that are needed to pollinate it,
also attracts me to propagate it.
    There are not that many places in the country where it can be found, but
woodland margins seem to be a favourite.

Snake's Head Fritillary. *Fritillaria meleagris.*
    Perennial. Moist soil.
The fascinating name means a 'dice box', the colour of the guinea hen, and
though I don't feel that it is a good description of the whole plant it does
show that the flower is made up of six checker-board patterned (purple/
black) petals, which are fused at their edges to form an angular box that is
held hanging upside down by the curved 8–24cm stem. It grows from a
well-buried bulb giving off a single flowering scape, flanked by alternate
thin, pointed leaves, with one, or sometimes two, flowers per plant at the
end during late spring. It grows, uncommonly, towards the South of
England, and especially in the low-lying Thames Valley.
    Plant this beauty 8cm deep in a bright, moist place in April, May or
June and don't worry about it being under grass, because it will fast
push its way through to flower. Divide away the offsets after it has withered
and replant them in autumn. It should be noticed that these bulbs are
poisonous and should be kept away from children. If you do not mind
waiting the 4–6 years to flowering time, plant the flat, pale yellow seeds in
August in a cold frame and prick them out in the second year.
    This appears to be such a beautiful plant that it has been picked in the
wild for such a long time that its numbers are going fast downhill, so
please help to stop the decline by growing your own.

ORCHIDS

There are very many species within the Orchis genus and many of them
were extremely common only 100 years ago but now we have reached the
situation where the natural habitats of these plants are disappearing and
they have become collectors' items. *Orchids in the wild should be left well
alone,* and it is for this reason that there are no cultivation details for either
of the species I mention – any nurseryman will tell you how it is done but

you'll probably have to buy a specimen from him to loosen his tongue. This at least means that if you grow them, there will be no need to take wild specimens.

The two examples I mention below are those that are generally pretty and more common than the others.

Early Purple Orchis. *Orchis mascula.*
Perennial. Damp soil, perhaps basic.
It grows from what at first sight looks like two tubers but in fact is a previous years one, withered and unused and a recent one, ovoid, harder and closer to the stem. This tuber sends up lanceolate leaves spotted on the stem side and about 24cm long. The stem, 12–40cm long ends up in a sort of 'tube cleaner brush' shaped head of purple flowers, which do not form a tapered mass as they do in many other orchids and are fairly widely spaced so you can see the stem between them – again unlike many other species. The petals form a shape difficult to describe and only seeing them in the wild will give you a clear view of them – try looking in open woods and damp meadows in the South of England. Each bloom starts off by exuding a very vanilla-like scent but soon, as it ages, this changes to a distinct cat smell, so over the April to June flowering period a definite change is perceived in the scent of a clump.

Seeds are brown and 0.3 × 0.2mm. There have been potions of aphrodisiac potency prepared from the Orchid, or so they say, so there is yet another good reason to try and grow it in the garden; after all surely it would be a better present for the wife than a bed of roses.

Common Spotted Orchis. *Orchis fuchsii.*
Perennial. Damp calcareous soil.
This grows about 60cm tall from a nobbled root – shaped a little like the fingers of a hand, which is used for perennation. The strong, thick stem is clothed by the pointed leaves, spotted on the upper surface, which diminish towards the flower head. This dense blaze of colour (in a range of shades from an albino version to a bright purple one) is spear-head shaped, the flowers being large towards the base and smaller towards the tip. Again the individual blooms need a real, true to life appreciation because of their oddity and they can be seen between May and August in damp chalky areas of open land. Just like the early purple it had many enemies in the form of snails, slugs, insects etc. and also the seeds are rarely seen, so it has a problem maintaining its numbers.

The Orchids have for a long time been subject to a good deal of gardening snobbery, which in a way is fairly reasonable because of the difficulties involved in their culture. Do not be put off – they need your help.

Low Creeping Plants for ground cover

(Roughly in the order of garden usefulness)

CRASSULACEAE. STONECROP FAMILY

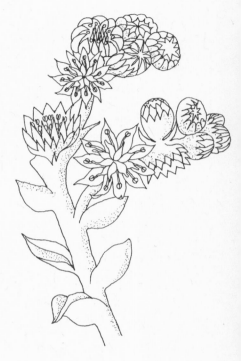

The Stonecrop Family is many and varied with great hordes of flowers that are already cultivated and some that are rare and neglected. The ones I give here are all candidates for the garden but it must be said that for the rarities you should always get them from your nurseryman rather than the natural habitat, which needs all the members it can get. Cultivation details are at the foot of the list.

Roseroot. *Sedum rosea.*
Perennial. Rocky places.
The 15–30cm stem of this holds the thick fleshy, pointed but broad leaves clustering their slightly greyish green way up to the expanse of dense flowers at the top. They form a yellow plateau, which is replaced by a red/orange one as the seeds form because of their intense crimson colour and indeed, as these stay in place for quite some time, it often looks as if the plant is still flowering well into the autumn whereas the real blooms are really only around between May and June. The thick rootstock and the stem both exude a rather rose-like scent when cut and for this reason no cottage garden would have been without it 100 years ago. Found mainly in Western Scotland, in its male and female forms.

Orpine. *Sedum telephium.*
Perennial. Woody places.
This is one of my favourites because it has the modesty to be a pretty and pink flower inside the woodland areas, whereas most flowers like this go and stand around in the sun. It is becoming quite rare now, but I'm sure that something can be done about that. It is a pink version of the rose root basically with the same kind of stem and flowers but pink in colour instead of yellow and with sparser leaves.
Flowers July to September but does not have pretty seeds.

Yellow Stone Crop. Wall Pepper. *Sedum acre.*
Perennial. Dry places.
It can carpet the place with its short (5–10cm) and fat leaved stems bearing the good old yellow stars at the head of each one. Just for the record they are about 1cm across with small red stamens and appear from the beginning of June to the end of July. The name Wall Pepper comes from the bitter, peppery taste of the leaves which were once used as a cure for ulcers, and this may be the reason why it has spread over all dry parts of the country so completely.

Rock Stone Crop. *Sedum forsterianum.*
Perennial. Rocky ground.
Just like the others except that its flowers make a rather less pointed star

and they may not be a flower on each stem, which is generally much taller than the others at its 15–30cm. June and July bring it out locally in Wales.

Large Yellow Stonecrop. *Sedum reflexum*.
Perennial. Rocky ground.

This is also a tall one being 15–25cm with its clusters of stalked, hanging in bud, yellow stars at the top. One nice thing is that you don't have to put up with all the dead leaves that persist on the stems in some species because there aren't any. June, July and August in Southern Britain generally.

English Stonecrop. *Sedum anglicum*.
Perennial. Rocky ground.

This is small and creeping with fleshy bitter, leaves with perhaps a tinge of pink growing up alternately on the 5cm stems. White petals in the familiar star-shape flowering all summer particularly on the western side of Great Britain but scattered all over the country. It has red fruits, which grow at the end of the short stalks that held the flowers.

White Stonecrop. *Sedum album*.
Perennial. Rocky ground.

A very similar plant to *Sedum anglicum* but larger, rarer and with more flowers.

Hairy Stonecrop. Pink Stonecrop. *Sedum villosum*.
Biennial. Damp rocky places.

Different from the others in having no barren stems, but is just the same shape, with the short stem, fleshy alternate leaves and the pink starry flowers. It is a rather rare plant which is found mainly in the border area between Scotland and England and flowers from June to August.

A common denominator if there ever was one is their bearing of poor soil gladly and the range that they will tolerate. Planting can take place in any part of the year, though actual new growth does not take place in winter. Division can similarly take place at almost any time though November to April are recommended. By the way, bits of leaves or almost any shoot will root readily in moist sand and in a way this is a problem because it allows them to spread easily. Water copiously during spring growth, less in summer but not in winter. Even summer periods of drought will hardly be noticed because of the moisture stores it has and, indeed, at one time there was the belief that it took water from the air.

Seeds can be sown March–April out of doors in sandy leafmould but vegetative propagation is much more satisfactory.

As wall coverings, edgings, house plants and alpines they all are extremely satisfactory as long as they get good sun.

POTENTILLAS

British potentillas (the name comes from Potens, which means powerful) are generally hardy affairs, low and creeping with similar yellow flowers. The selection here has been made to suit a range of habitat and to give a widely differing bunch because there are many very similar members of the group.

Cultivation is usually easy (see Marsh Cinquefoil, p. 98) and control is simple, purely by weeding out unwanted plants. Habitat is taken to be sunny spots on dryish ground unless stated below.

Potentilla species are all small creepers.

Silverweed. *Potentilla anserina.*
Perennial. Ordinary soil.
This is a low creeper, a bit difficult to control but not so vigorous as would endanger fairly strong neighbours. It grows up to about 10cm with runners spreading out about 30cm with silvery leaves alternating one large, one small along the thin stems and forming a silvery mat (this is at least true with those varieties with the silvering on the top of the leaves as this is not always the case). It is found in damp, grassy and waste places throughout Britain. It flowers all summer with stalked yellow 3cm flowers.

There have been medicinal uses for this one for thousands of years with its treatments for ulcers and sores, and to keep the feet comfortable on walks. A flour was once made out of the roots as was a porridge.

Shrubby Cinquefoil. *Potentilla fruticosa.*
Perennial. Limestone or chalk soil.
This is a bushy affair 30–90cm tall growing all over the British Isles but rare. It has pretty five-petalled flowers (male and female separately).

Give it light soil and a sunny spot when planting, which should be in either spring or autumn. It can be propagated easily by taking 10–12cm cuttings of non-flowering, fresh growth shoots in late spring and potting them in sandy loam under glass. Plant these out in summer.

Tormentil. *Potentilla erecta.*
Perennial. Acid soils.
A dainty but fairly long-stemmed plant that often grows prostrate but does not root from the stems. The yellow flowers on fairly long stalks have four petals usually (and may have five) but they don't manage to outshine the predominant green of the leaves and the whole plant looks very herby. It was used as a treatment for diarrhoea in children and the roots give a red dye which was used instead of the tannin from the oak bark. It is found in light soil in grasslands growing 22–30cm high all over Great Britain.

Hoary Cinquefoil. *Potetentilla argentea.*
Perennial. Sandy or gravelly soil.
This is a smaller plant which may grow upwards and sideways much like Tormentil with small flowers.

Creeping Cinquefoil. *Potentilla reptans.* Twice the size of:
Trailing Tomentil. *Potentilla anglica.*
Perennials. Non-calcareous soils.
They creep around with long rooting stems and palmate, long petioled leaves and individually stalked, 4 petalled yellow flowers 15mm across. They are generally found most easily in England but are widespread.

Sulphur Cinquefoil. *Potentilla recta.*
Biennial. Light soil.
A 22–45cm plant, thriving in hot wastes, growing from its 2.2 × 1.5mm seeds to flower in its first year with large (up to 2cm) five-petalled primrose-coloured flowers at the top of the wiry stem. It is rare at the moment in Central and Southern England but is in no danger. Possibly perennial in the right conditions.

Marsh Cinquefoil. *Potentilla palustris.*
    Perennial. Marsh boggy soil.
I do not know why this one is so highly travelled but it has spread from Siberia and North America all over the northern hemisphere in the temperate climate. It has purple petals and long sepals forming the striking and memorable heads at the summit of 15–45cm stems.

    Gardened once around pond margins and boggy places it appears to have gone out of vogue leaving it and its creeping rhizome to go back to its wild habitat of the North and Scotland.

    Leaving aside the shrubby Cinquefoil, all the Potentillas here have the same cultive method, though please adapt it to suit the habitat of each plant. Planting should take place in October/November or March/April in deep, rich, well drained, loamy soil in partial shade or full sun. Division – a process requiring care – should be in October, by dividing up rhizomatous pieces into rooted parts. Seeds planted in loamy soil in March or April, should be under glass (or later out of doors) and about 2cm apart (they are quite large – 2 × 2mm usually), thinning as they germinate. The group contains some like Silverweed that is delightful as just ground cover and others like Marsh Cinquefoil with lovely flowers, so there is a good range to choose from here.

CISTACEAE. ROCK ROSE FAMILY

I think for the Rock Rose family I should better only advise specifically about one type because all the British ones apart from that are only found in very localized areas and might thank me (and you) for leaving them alone. Anyway they will get a mention because they're so nice to look at.

Common Rock Rose. *Helianthemum chamaeastus*
    Perennial. Calcareous, light soil, but also in acid soil.
I'm sure that everyone will have seen this or its garden forms already, but just for the record, it is a creeping, rooting-as-it-goes, low, woody plant with yellow flowers growing on short stems and coming out from June to mid-August. It likes a dry sunny position and has a very mobile flower with petals opening with the sun and stamens folding back to the touch. It can be a disappointment in dull weather because the flowers may not open at all and the only colour being the red tinges to the stems and leaves, but in general it has enough light to bother opening. The name *Helianthemum* means 'sun flower' so you can see that this is one of the dominant features. It grows on chalk and limestone areas of Britain but it has been reported as having the time of its life on acid Scottish soil.

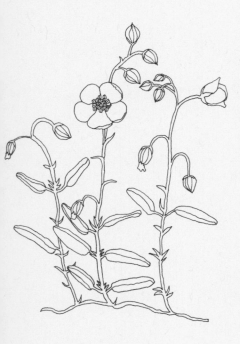

    The White Rock Rose from Weston-Super-Mare is a rather more silvery version.

    The Hairy Rock Rose, a silvery grey forming round shrub mats, hairy all over and found in the Falway Bay area.

    The Common Rock Rose can hybridize with both of these varieties but I think it is better on its own.
Annual Rock Rose. *Helianthemum guttatum.* A rare seaside plant that flowers for a few weeks in the beginning of May.

    All of them appear to have albino versions, and are cultivated like the Common Rock Rose. Not surprisingly from what I have been saying, both the Rock Rose and its close relatives, need a culture method based on the sun, and this means cosseting throughout the year with the sunniest place in the garden as its summer home. Although nominally perennial, they tend not to last more than 3 years as good plants, so their culture apart from just division is quite important.

Plant in spring where they are to bloom in the summer and either transplant to pots in autumn, to spend the winter under glass or protect them out of doors with glass sheeting or boxes. Wintering in the cold frame, I find the most satisfactory because it means that there are then fewer things to worry about, being bitten by frost. Seeds, which are 2.0 × 1.5mm and black, should be planted in separate pots under glass in mid-spring, hardened off as the weather improves and planted out in late spring. A better method of propagation, I believe is through cuttings of young shoots taken in the summer and planted into sand to root (7cm apart in cold frame). It is a real shame, but some blooms may only last one day – leaving plenty more, mind you – and very decorative too.

Mountain Avens. *Dryas octopetala.*
Perennial. Calcareous soil.
This is a creeping perennial, growing 7–15cm tall with its dense, woody stems and tufts of hairy, crinkly simple leaves from the base of the flowering cape, which is also covered with hairs, though they're darker here. The 30–35mm, eight-petalled flowers are around from June until August and are a flawless white converging on a bunch of yellow stamens. It is evergreen and that must help it a bit in the highland districts where it is normally found (rare).

This Arctic import can be planted in very moisture retentive (much compost or leafmould) though limey or sandy soil in September/October or April, in sheltered semi-shade. The only exception to thise is the planting out of pot-grown plants, which can be at any time providing the weather is good. Once planted it should be left alone, rooted branches, from spring layering, being taken off the side or cuttings of new growth taken in summer, because, like seedlings the roots are easily damaged. Cuttings can be rooted in sand and planted out gently in October.

Seeds should be sown in pans of fine soil with a little peat added, in April or May, and this should be done thinly with only a light soil covering to make sure that little thinning is needed. Plant out the seedlings very gently, and about 10cm apart, assuming that some will not stand up to the transplantation and effectively thin out the population a little further. Flowering comes in the second year. Sometimes, I get the distinct impression that God has turned off the central heating in our country and seeing this 'Frozen North' plant living happily through it all, does at least mean that something doesn't mind. A rock garden is the ideal place for it.

Ivy-leaved Toadflax. *Cymbalaria muralis.*
Perennial. Old Walls.
A well-respected garden plant of the early seventeenth century it was introduced into Britain just for that purpose but has spread all over the country since that time, to decorate any dry wall or dry ground that will take it. It is a creeping plant with long trailing stems up to 100cm long, branching as it grows and giving off paired very ivy-like leaves and the typical Toadflax flowers 5mm across with a yellow tongue to the otherwise purple dragon flowers, which can be seen from mid-May to mid-September. Don't worry about its ability to climb up any wall you care to put it near because the stems seem to seek out convenient cracks and hang onto them. Bees like it.

Just a few details about the horticulture should suffice, it being such an amenable plant to a variety of conditions. Plant it while fairly young in either autumn or spring in a partially shaded place where it has access to plenty of root moisture so that it doesn't have to waste its energy searching out water for its fast growing shoots. Walls are the best places to show it off en masse but it will hang nicely from a basket or creep along the ground fairly easily as well. Sow the 0.8 × 0.6mm minute grey seeds in pots in spring under good light, uncovered and plant out as soon as they are about 12cm tall. Division and cuttings are possible, in the usual way but seeds produce excellent results.

Round-leaved Fluellen. *Kickxia spuria*.
Annual. Light chalk or sandy soil.

A creeping ivy-like affair, not much dissimilar to Ground Ivy at first sight, with greener pinnate leaves and a 12–25cm stem giving off the short flower pedicels at nodes. The flowers, which come out, from July to October are about 10mm across, and are brown and yellow. It is most likely to be found in South-East England and Wales, where there is sand or chalky soil.

It is a rather rare plant that can be propagated most satisfactorily by seed, in the soil detailed above, sown in autumn to germinate the following year. Fairly effective ground cover with a few bright flowers is formed by planting in half shade and about 15cm apart.

Sharp-leaved Fluellen. *Kickxia elatine*.
Annual. Any soil.

This appears to be the Northern counterpart of *Kickxia spuria*, being a little less hairy, slightly larger and not flowering as long (July to September).

Wild Thyme. *Thymus drucei*.
Perennial. Dryish chalky soil.

An evergreen plant usually that will form carpets of itself over the poorest of soils, and in fact there have been times in which lawns have been made of it. The famous sweet Thyme smell is represented in it very markedly through the effects of the granular dots on the leaves, which exude the scent. As for flowers they are held above the low horizontal stems by 5–10cm leafy (the leaves are small and glossy) stem branches and they form white/crimson clusters from late June to mid-August. Each individual bloom is about 5mm across and makes a sweet nectar. It appears to like warm coastal areas, particularly in the West where it is found in poor, chalky soils, waste land, and mountainous regions. A tea was made from it which was purported to give great strength and courage, and an essential oil with particular fragrance could be extracted though the Larger Wild Thyme was the usual plant for this.

To preserve the Thyme cut it in high summer, before it has flowered, on the morning of a dry sunny day, gather it into bunches and hang them up to dry. The culinary version is *Thymus vulgaris*, a very similar plant indeed.

It is incredibly easy to grow, the best forms coming direct from the 1mm seed, sown in April in light soil and thinned to about 12cm. It grows like lightning and lawns can be made of it in one year. Being an evergreen makes it a good lawn plant, so plant the seedlings out 30cm apart in May, leave it for about three months, by which time there should be no room left bare. Divide the low stems up into separately rooted pieces and plant them 15cm apart on the lawn-to-be. By winter you will have a solid green expanse, which should receive some sand to consolidate it.

SPEEDWELLS

Of the Speedwells none is particularly spectacular, they just make useful ground cover with some bright blue four-petalled flowers.

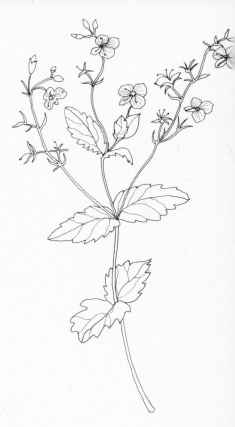

Field Speedwell. *Veronica persica.*
  Annual. Ordinary soil.
Just to show you how good this plant is at filling all the ecological niches it can, may I point out that it was unrecorded in Britain until 1825 and since then has become a very common plant of any soil, in low grassy meadows all over the country. From short fibrous roots grows a decumbent stem base, which gives off similarly brown side shoots and leafy flowering stems, which rarely get over 18cm tall. The production of the bright eyed 1cm flowers goes on from early March to late October, but each bloom does not last long. There are similar ground spreaders including *Veronica officinalis*, which is the Common Speedwell of copse and woodland, which can also be recommended. For cultivation follow the seed directions of the next species, and use it as ground cover at lawn edges because although it self seeds, mowing removes it eventually.

Germander Speedwell or **Bird's eye.** *Veronica chamaedrys.*
  Perennial. Ordinary soil.
This is a rather larger, more vertical affair than the last plant, with a 18–24cm stem ending in a spike of blue flowers (or occasionally white one) flowering in succession from early May to mid-June. Diagnostic features of it are the two lines of hairs going up the stem, the broadish nettle-like leaves that can be made into a tea and a stem that may harbour a harmless gall fly. It can be found in grassy, shady locations throughout Britain, or sown to clothes to ward off accident.
  Sow seeds in March in a cold frame, ordinary soil and uncovered, planting out in a sunny well-drained location as soon as large enough. Unearth and replant every other year to prevent a clump becoming overcrowded. Both plants are very easy to grow.

Yellow Pimpernel. *Lysimachia nemorum.*
  Perennial, Herbaceous. Any light soil.
A pretty little plant with rather small flowers, so it is not one of the garden favourites, but is nice enough to be allowed into a few wastes with nothing better to put in them – if only because it is easy to grow. Commonly found all over Britain, likes moist woods and wet spaces with a little shade.
  The blooms are 14–16mm across and sow seeds that are rather hard to get hold of.
  It is a small, low creeper, very much like a Scarlet Pimpernel with yellow flowers. Use the same cultivation method as for Scarlet Pimpernel (p. 102).

Creeping Jenny. *Lysimachia nummularia.*
  Perennial. A creeping, low plant. Moist ground.
At one time there was a trade from Australia in this plant because of its beautiful golden yellow, almost buttercup-like flowers, which are spread along the creeping plant. The 5–61cm stems creep and root as they go and this appears to be its main method of propagation as it has never in Britain been known to seed. The bright cupped flowers are on short stalks with five petals and five sepals producing scraps of the colour wherever it gets a hold. (June–August.) For some odd reason it may only flower in years of

drought and it may be advisable to put it in a place that partially dries out in summer. Found all over the country in shady moist places.

Forget the seed method of growing Yellow Loosestrife and look at the vegetative methods. In a way even that isn't necessary because it can be divided at any time of the year by simply chopping the stem into segments and planting each rooted piece separately in the moist, shady places it prefers. There are huge expanses of it in places and this demonstrates just how easily it spreads vegetatively, though there is no seed spread to guard against. Of course seeds are available from abroad but it is so easy to fill the garden without them that there hardly seems much point in buying them. Lastly it may be nice to know that it will keep down many fast-growing weeds so plant it anywhere you're having trouble.

Scarlet Pimpernel. *Anagallis arvensis.*
    Annual. A creeping herb. Dry ground, any soil.
The poor man's weather glass as it is called in some parts of the country because its petals close at night and during damp weather so it is a useful sign of impending rain. It creeps along the ground and will cover any space offered because of the fast growth. Cultivated ground usually has it some-where and it is common throughout the British Isles on waste ground and any bare ground as the first new occupant in the vacant situation. It is a pity but the long flowering period, usually all summer, is made up for by the usually small numbers of flowers out at one time, which may be red, blue or white. Behind the prettiness there is a little bit that is sinister; the black dots on the leaves exude a substance to which many people are allergic.

Horticulturally here is hardly any problem. Seeds (2×1mm brown) being sown where they are to bloom in March in well-drained light soil in a sunny position. The method I prefer is to plant the seeds in pans under glass in early March, let the seedlings get to a fair size (thinning as neces-sary) and then plant them out in clumps in places needing ground cover, in the rockery or as a path edging. This way they cannot be confused with some very similar weeds.

Bog Pimpernel. *Anagalis tenella.*
    Perennial. A creeping herb. Ordinary soil.
Creeps along with its thin and delicate stems and pretty, small pink flowers rooting as it goes. The flowers are on small stalks, they have five pointed petals and the yellow anthers stick out between them. Being found mainly in the wet western areas of the country, it appears to like a lot of moisture though even this does not prevent them from being difficult to establish in the garden. Flowers between June and August.

Once it has got a hold of the ground, then the best way to propagate is by division of the rooting stem into many rooted segments in March. Initial planting should be in Spring in damp, slightly acidic soil in partial shade and a warm part of the garden.

Seeds can be treated as the Scarlet Pimpernel, though a generally warmer approach is needed. Guard this plant from the attentions of other fast creepers that like the same kind of soil, *Lysimachia nummularia* for instance, because in any battle it will come off worst.

Cloudberry. *Rubus chamaemorus.*
    Perennial. Peaty, moist soil.
This is a 15cm creeping version of the blackberry, with very similar, but orange fruits and the same kind of 5–6 petalled flowers. It thrives in

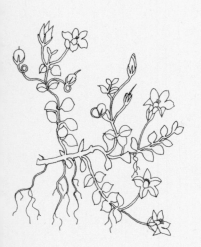

moor and bog, peaty soils generally, high up and as a result is found in the middle of the Pennines and Scottish Highlands. It is a low creeper, with spreading underground stems and simple flowering stems, which bear the 25–30mm flowers from the middle of June to the end of July.

Planting can take place from the end of autumn right through to the middle of spring as it starts to stir from the winter dormancy. The soil should be pretty poor but humus-filled and moist, though well drained. Division of the root stock can take place in March and layering, the other vegetative method I'll consider, happening after the shoots have started growing (i.e. peg a shoot to the soil so that once new growth begins, a set of roots will form at its base).

Seeds can go into the same type of soil in autumn or spring and, as it is fairly hardy, I recommend autumn so as to get earlier flowering the following year. These seeds should be put where it is to flower in a sunny spot.

Shrubs and climbers
(Roughly in order of garden usefulness)

Honeysuckle. Woodbine. *Lonicera periclymenum.*
Perennial. Woody. Any soil.
Georgeous stuff. If you have not got it already it doesn't take long to start repaying efforts to introduce it. A tall woody climber (180cm easily) it winds its way around whatever it can lay its stem against and crawls up following the direction of the sun around the support. Masses of pinnate leaves turn it into a 'joy forever' and during the whole of the summer the clusters of long, thin, snap-dragon-shaped flowers come out. They start off as cream elongated buds and open to allow the moths to be attracted by the very strong sweet fragrance to pollinate them. After fertilisation the flowers yellow and wither, leaving berries and seed. If you take off the flowers in its prime and pull out the stamens, which loop out through its mouth, then it should be possible to suck the nectar out of the flower base; it is sweet and scented. Honeysuckle is found all over Britain and has been a symbol to avert evil powers on May Day for many years along with being the 'flower of love' to Shakespeare.

Its latin name comes from that of a German botanist Adam Lonicer (1528–86) and I'm sure he'd be pleased if he knew. A well drained but moisture-retentive soil is best for planting and should receive the plant in either October or March. Cuttings from a good plant can be taken in the summer (make sure that it's new growth with no flowers) and rooted in sand, this taking a few weeks. Plant out the rooted cutting in a cold frame with sandy loam and leave it until the spring. Allow full growth to set in and then, when it has started to slow down towards the end of spring cut it back to 20cm to ensure good strong roots. After that treatment it should withstand anything. Other methods of increasing the stock involve layering from August to November and separating the rooted twig from its parent or sowing seed in gentle heat (55–60°F) from February to March and gradually hardening off.

The seed itself is 4 × 2.5mm and should be set in rich soil, about 1cm down and 6cm from its neighbour. Prune the adult plant any time after

flowering or early spring. Watch out for it strangling other plants and give it something strong to climb up – a trellis perhaps.

Please don't get taken in by the artificial varieties, often they are scentless and, outside shows, much less attractive.

WILD ROSES

For cultivation see under sweet briar

Dog Rose. *Rosa canina.*
Perennial. Any soil.
Just what you would expect from a wild rose, the long, hooked thorns, the pinnate leaves and the tall straggliness that takes it up to eight metres tall over any object that it can find. The flowers come out in little bunches in June and July, being pink and white with a sweet scent but not nectar. The blooms are 50–80mm across dying to leave their receptacle as a bright red hip, which contains the achenes, collected during the last war for their high vitamin C content. It was learned very early in gardening history, that this rose's stock is resistant, as are most of the wild varieties, to the ailments that beset the imported roses and their hybrids, so the Dog Rose has become the root stock of most garden roses. It is spread out all over the British Isles in hedges and thickets on any soil, straggling over anything that happens to get in the way.

Burnet Rose. *Rosa spinosissima.*
Perennial. Rocky ground.
Found in coastal and rocky areas, mountain ledges and dunes it appears to like good drainage. The strong rootstock gives out a 12–120cm stem with the usual rose leaves and the thorns to bear up high the 30–40mm flower with five petals facing out like a fold away flash-gun reflector and the pretty centre of yellow stamens. Coming out from May to September, the flowers may in fact be white, yellow or pink or, indeed, any mixture of these, each leaving behind after their time has gone 12mm purple black fruits. Watch out for those suckers.

Field Rose. *Rosa arvensis.*
Perennial. Rich soil.
It forms a low spreading bush by an amassing of the spreading stems that just flop over anything that is around to lean on. It is very much like the Burnet Rose in description except that it is bigger and more strongly built with perhaps fewer prickles but stronger ones and hooked. The all-important flowers are usually white, from 30–45mm in diameter on the same format as the Burnet but from the beginning of June to the end of July. Found in deciduous woodland in England and Wales generally.

Downy Rose. *Rosa villosa.*
Perennial. Any soil.
This is very similar to the Dog Rose in many ways but is shorter, being up to 180cm at the outside in height, and with smaller deeper pink flowers (30–50mm dia.), which are much longer lasting. It is found in Northern England and Scotland.

Sweet Briar. *Rosa rubiginosa.*
  Perennial. Chalky soil.
Woods, hedges, and scrub give us this pink flowered shrub (it can be white, but rarely), which gives off a sweet scent all over the leaf surfaces as well as having fragrant flowers. It grows up to 90cm on chalky soil in the Eastern Counties mainly, but it is found all over the British Isles as well.

In a short book like this I could not possibly aim to put in all the details that have been written about rose cultivation over the years. All I can say is that wild roses should be given the same treatment as garden types except that pruning can be harder; suckers will be of the same type of rose as you have already and that all the cosseting and pampering is rarely needed. To obtain your specimens you could just take suckers from old and dying garden roses because these will usually be of dog rose.

Hop. *Humulus lupulus.*
  Perennial. Ordinary soil.
I do not think any book on wild flowers can possibly bypass such an important plant as this. After all it has been used to make beer since the sixteenth century, before which many other herbs were used, (nettles for instance). In fact it is the female flowers that are used in the process, with their scaly 2cm pineapple shape and not the male ones, which are on a separate plant and rather uninteresting. This climber will scale anything, with its hairy stem that holds on tight and gives off broad, serrated tri- or unilobed leaves on the way to its maximum of about five metres. The flowers, which are fragrant when dry, with a slight narcotic effect (hence it is put in pillows, for the insomniac, and said to give a deep sleep) are around from July to September and give 6mm nutlets as they wither.
  Agriculturally few male plants are wanted (though some are needed to fertilise the female flowers, which then produce the lupulin – the resin wanted by the brewers) so vegetative reproductive methods are used. The aerial stems are annual so at the end of the season, as they die off, their bases swell with the food from the involuting stems. Cut off these short underground remainders in autumn and put them into damp nursery bed soil, where they will quickly produce roots. Transplant to the final site in the spring, giving plenty of manure, food soil, freedom from excessive wind and something to climb. The original specimen can be obtained through agricultural suppliers, from a local farmer or through seeds of wild plants, which, despite giving fifty percent male plants, will prove useful. I think that planting them in spring, where they are to grow would be the best way but it will be the second year before a good show is seen.

PAPILIONACEAE (PEA FAMILY)

Dyer's Greenweed. *Genista tinctoria.*
  Perennial. Sandy, clay soil.
It got its name from being used as a green/yellow dye for a few centuries, but was phased out with the introductions of much faster dyes and synthetics. It tends to deplete the soil when grown as a crop because of its high rate of growth and because the number of crops per year is high. It is a bushy affair, frail and thornless, growing rarely taller than 30cm from deep strong roots. The leaves and flowers are very much like broom but the yellow flowers are in long spikes. I have not actually grown this myself and

also there appears to be confusion in the textbooks as to the nature of the correct soil – they just cannot agree, but from the sites that it is found in the wild I should say sandy or clay soil suits it best.

It is a pretty plant that could easily be given a place in a border and its culture is certainly easy enough to prevent it from being a problem. Plant it between October and March in a sunny position (don't forget that it must still be a sunny spot once the leaves have arrived on the trees) and about 15cm apart. To propagate take cuttings during summer of fresh growth and root them in sand. The side shoots are the best for cuttings and they are in turn best in either April or August. A better way to increase numbers is through seed planted either as soon as it is ripe out of doors or under glass in early spring. This should be done in light loamy soil and in pans so that seedlings can be planted out as soon as they are a few inches tall. Clip the plants after they have flowered to keep them in shape, and perhaps you might get rid of the quickly spreading seeds this way too.

Broom. *Sarothamnus scoparius.*
Perennial. Lime free soil.

The name Broom comes from the fact that it has been used as the sweeping utensil for years, this because it keeps the flexibility of its stems and is largely leafless (the stems act like the leaves of a normal plant).

It managed to give the 'plantagenet' name to the line of kings, from being worn in the king's cap. A tall (90–180cm) plant it grows with an angular and spineless stem to give showers of yellow snapdragon flowers (which are sometimes tinged with orange from the reflection of the pollen in the 'throat') from May until August. It is found in dry places all over the British Isles in many colours, is slightly scented and on the Highlands, where it managed to give an emblem to the Forbes clan, it still produces marvellous honey. As a herb the flower buds can be used like capers and it makes a good diuretic.

When Linnaeus (one of the fathers of modern botany) first saw this plant he 'fell to his knees and thanked God for its loveliness'.

Plant in spring before growth restarts, in poor gravelly soil with no lime. This is possible for small plants but once they get fairly large they won't stand interference with their roots. Keep the shoots in check by pruning after the flowers have gone in autumn, but be careful not to take away anything but new growth because it will discourage growth the next year. Seeds can be sown broadcast and left uncovered during early spring in an open, sunny site, or they can be sown in 7cm pots and planted out selectively.

Gorse, Furze or Whin. *Ulex europaeus.*
Perennial. Poorish lime-free soil.

This anti-witch shrub grows from strong roots a thick woody stem which may become bare at the bottom with time and so does not make everlasting hedging, grows up to three metres tall with its much-branched spiny stem and small dark-green leaves. The flowers are 15–20mm in diameter, a striking yellow and exude a peppery sweet smell in April and June – though it continues sporadically for the rest of the year as well. It is a very hardy species that thrives in lime-free soils but if they are too rich then it becomes leggy and ceases to be compact and manageable. Gorse grows on heaths, commons, roadsides, and hedges and will live for a very long time.

The three species of *Ulex* that I have detailed here have roughly the same cultivation method as that of broom, except they will put up with clipping a lot more easily.

Lesser Gorse. *Ulex minor.*
    Perennial. Lime free soil.
A compact, less spiny, smaller flowered, less scented version of gorse. To be found on waste land in the East of England mainly. Flowers from July to September.

Western Gorse. *Ulex gallii.*
    Perennial. Acid soil.
Absolutely intermediate between the previous two types. Found in the West Country mainly.

Small Bindweed, Field Bindweed. *Convulvulus arvensis.*
    Has many local names: Hardy perennial, herbaceous creeper.
Found almost everywhere in Britain except mountainous areas, a climbing, straggling plant, that needs others for its scaffolding, often the brown, dry, curly remnant is left in winter after its support has been withdrawn by the weather. Leaves spiral up the long stems, which grow just about as long as is necessary to get them into the light and about two feet from the ground. Pink and white segmented flowers like parasols that close at night and exude a rich nectar and a sweet almond scent. Flowering June–September (longer in warm weather) and its black pea-sized capsules full of small black seeds can be harvested about two weeks after the flowers have dropped. This is a really powerful plant; once it is going it is quite hard to stop the thing from taking over. Keep the tall plants away, and no roses for at least four feet because it will get to them if it can. Give the plant a lattice or a wall to play with and you will get a persistent sweet-smelling show all summer, and a green fence that does not molest nearby plants. Almost any soil will do, though it used to be a sign of a good gravel bed underneath, but watch out: once the long, deep rhizomes get a hold they will take a lot of getting rid of. That is why, by the way, it is often included in garden flower books – because it just will not go.

    Plant 5cm pieces of rhizome (including a node) 7–15cm down (it isn't critical as it's bound to come through anyway). Any time up to May will do as they are pretty hardy.
    Seeds are not a particularly convenient way of growing them because of the uncertainty of germination and their vulnerability to being overrun by weeds. Still, if you can find capsules, plant their seeds about 5mm down and 15cm apart outside in April and May or grow seedlings in ordinary garden soil but under glass and plant out around them.

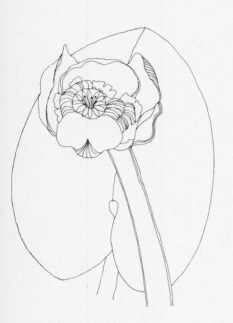

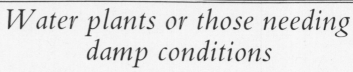

Water plants or those needing damp conditions

(Roughly in order of garden usefulness)

THE LILY FAMILY

Yellow Waterlily. *Nuphar lutea.*

Perennial. Pools, slow rivers.

This slow water lover with large tough round leaves, on long stalks from the roots in the mud at the bottom, floating on the surface of the water, seems to do best where it isn't too deep. The flowers are held above the water by stems and what looks to us casually to be the petals, but we find them, in fact, to be large yellow sepals leaving the many petals to be small and cover the inside of the cup. Smelling of stale wine from the ethyl acetate the flowers bloom from June to September being 40–50mm in diameter and drop their seeds into the water.

The name Nuphar comes from the old arabic word for the plant – Naufar. Plant in October or March under water more than two feet deep in a lily basket that holds a rich soil and lower them into the pool. Divide its roots as the rhizomes finish their winter dormancy in March.

Sow seeds under water into heavy soil and plant them out directly into deep water when they have reached about 30cm tall. A good place for them is full sun in water that is either still or slow moving. See also white water lily for further cultivation points.

White Waterlily. *Nymphaea alba.*

Perennial. Very slow or still water.

Yes, this is the Japanese emblem of purity and in fact this plant has spread right round the world as an ornament. This too, has the thick, tough, floating leaves anchored to the bottom by the long petioles but it differs in that the flower too has to float. A smashing white affair with many pointed petals curving round the outside of a dense bunch of bright yellow stamens, with white (inside) and green (outside) sepals going around the petals in turn. The whole flower being 10–12cm diameter and coming out from June to August just to release a 4cm berry which sinks and gradually decays on the bottom of the pool, scattering the seeds in the process. When it is flowering, hope for some sunshine because the flower, and indeed the whole plant, rides higher in the water and opens out as the sun shines. Not only does it look fabulous but in Greece, a cordial is made from the leaves and flowers.

Plant in spring before the growth starts. One of the best methods is to put the tubers in a wicker basket, cover with good compost-rich soil to a depth of about 20cm and cover that with sand to prevent it from floating away. Set it in about 30cm of water but during the whole process make sure that the roots do not dry out and watch out to prevent the leaves curling, once they are out of the water, by keeping them moist. Using this method it will be necessary to replant them every 3–4 years because the soil will be exhausted, although a fertiliser wrapped in clay and cheesecloth can be dropped around the roots to extend soil-richness.

Propagation can be by division just before regrowth starts in March. Unlike the cultivated varieties this is true from seed, so by planting in spring in pans at 60°F under 2cm of sand and 6cm of water, new plants can be grown. When floating leaves have been produced transplant them into separate pots and plant out either that October or the following spring.

Yellow Flag. *Iris pseudacorus.*
Perennial. Shallow water.
This plant is the Fleur de Lys of France, and is thus spread widely throughout Western Europe. It grows from bulbous rootstock, which spreads very quickly by the stout rhizomes as a tall plant (up to 5 feet in good conditions) with long pointed swords of leaves and a flowering stem which bears a succession of flowers from May to August. The flower is typical of the flag irises, though a bright yellow and very eyecatching, because it must catch the bee's eye because self pollination is prevented. The seeds were roasted to make a coffee-like drink, the root gave a black dye and the whole plant was supposed to be able to avert evil.

Exactly the same can be said about its cultivation as was said about the Gladdon (p. 60) except that the plant, being so fond of water, may prove difficult to divide or even restrain. I suggest planting it initially at the edge of any pool, so that its progress can be checked at any time and of course it makes life much easier, i.e. plant the tubers only a few inches down and in a maximum of 7cm of water, in winter. Note here that unlike many garden flowers there is no storing of the roots, no need for winter protection, because it is quite hardy, as most British plants have to be.

Monkeyflower. *Mimulus guttatus.*
Perennial. Very damp places.
This is a naturalized garden escape that came originally from the Aleutian Islands for the landscape garden market in the early nineteenth century. It appears to have travelled by canal from the place where it first got a taste of wild living, Wales, into England and has since bedded down for good. It is a very beautiful yellow flower that grows with its fleshy leaves and thick, typical-of-water-plants, light greenstem, in shallow still or running water throughout the wet parts of Britain; West and North England and East Scotland. The two centimetre Antirrhinum type flowers have a whole leash of red dots on the lower petal and when a heavy insect lands here, it causes the flower to close up (once it has pollinated the flower) this is so that the flower does not self pollinate. Flowers mid-June to mid-August.

In autumn it may get straggly – rake off the excess. Could you ever want easier propagation? Layering and picking off rooted stems is pretty easy; do it in spring. Cuttings of non-flowering stems can be taken during summer and put into damp soil until well rooted and planted out. Alternatively they should form good roots if just left in water!

Arrowhead. *Sagittaria sagittifolia.*
Perennial. Shallow still, or running water.
A water plant that creeps away from its original blue and yellow tubers with rooting stems. It sends up a robust 60–90cm spike of widely spaced, three-petalled 2cm purple-centred flowers, which are white for the most part and last from early July to mid-August. It is found mainly in the Midlands and South-East England in ponds and canals, and it may have been spread along by the passage of the narrow boats. At one time a tea was made out of the very pointed arrowhead shaped fleshy leaves that are held above the water by the same ribbed type of stem that holds the flowers.

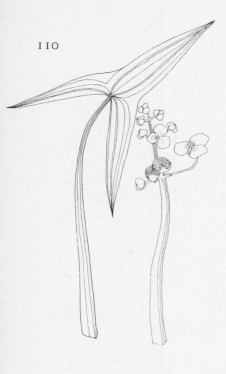

Horticulturally a small book could be written about just this one plant so here I'll detail the optimum times and conditions for action and just tell you that large variations can be made as long as the general principle is not forgotten. In planting, set the stock tubers horizontally in a heavyish loam, which is slightly acid. Those tubers, which are a food in the Far East, should be about 7cm into the soil and in about 15cm of water, which should not be stagnant. A good way to do this process easily is to pot them and then sink the pots (or preferably tubs), but this will make repotting every three or four years necessary as that soil (about 30 cubic cm per plant) becomes exhausted. When dividing the stock, remember that each year a new tuber is formed so that any old tubers can be discarded. Divide in spring.

The seed method is, I believe, preferable to the rather mucky division, and consists of removing the seeds from the red berries soon after ripening and planting them in boxes of salty, heavy soil. They should be 5cm down and transplanted into either a tub or the pool bed, either when they are big enough seedlings or after the first year. The seeds will spread it round any pool naturally, and as a controlling measure it is wise to remove the berries though it is easy to remove excess shoots and plants in early summer, simply by pulling.

Look out for a pretty double variety that has much larger flowers than normal.

Yellow Loosestrife. *Lysimachia vulgaris.*
Perennial. A water plant. Damp ground, any soil.
The scientific name comes from Lysimachos, the ancient King of Thrace, though the connection between them is a little tenuous. It is a tall (122cm) upstanding and strong plant, with paired leaves up among the flowers and a decumbent rooting system growing from the horizontal base of the stem. The flowers, which are arranged on the upper third of the stem as a pyramid, have five yellow petals and five red stamens opposite them and are about 2cm across with an almost bell-like shape. They come out in July and August with little scent and produce 2 × 1.5mm yellow seeds. Found all over Great Britain they clump together at the edge of the water, liking well-drained lowlands or damp humus-rich soil.

I cannot understand why there are such weird and wonderful recipes for the soil this plant needs; one I have seen even includes coconut fibres! Let me reassure you that rich, moist, porous soil is good enough to get this growing well. Planting should be in damp ground in spring or autumn, division of the rootstock, which is a good way to increase the number of clumps can be done at the same time.

Seeds are produced and should be grown in pans of sandy loam, by being planted 5mm deep in early spring and planted out as soon as tall enough (make sure that each seedling is about 5cm from the next). It spreads fairly fast especially if it is in its favourite shady-type spot but I cannot see anyone complaining with a flower show like that.

Marsh Marigold or Kingcup. *Caltha palustris.*
Perennial. Herbaceous. Slightly acid heavy soil.
This has been around in Britain a long time because evidence of it is found in pre-ice age sediments and this is a pretty good indication of just how hardy this water or marsh plant is. It has long white roots that anchor it in place, a thick, hollow 15–45cm stem with thick large, rounded, fleshy leaves and, from March to mid-May is capped by the large (4cm) golden

flowers. I am sorry to say it yet again but the flowers, though extremely large and unmissable are distinctly buttercup-shaped and green centred, producing 3.5 × 3.0mm brown elongated seeds. If you look hard you will come across the albino and double forms of the flower which may have to be propagated vegetatively. It grows strongly in all parts of the British Isles in fresh water and any place which can supply enough moisture may well end up covered by it.

The name comes from the Greek 'Kalathos' which means goblet and describes the shape of the flowers. Plant in autumn in mucky soil well supplied by water but not stagnant. The soil should be on the acid side of neutrality, but not too acid and may be anything really from the heavy soil described above to sandy loam. Each individual plant will need to be about 45cm from the next because of the rate of growth of the fleshy, edible leaves and stems, and it should be in a place to receive winter sun, summer shade and protection from the drying East wind. Divide the shoots into separately rooted pieces in spring in damp weather to decrease the change of drying the pieces out. To me anyway seeds are just a long way of achieving the same result as can be obtained more easily.

Propagate by division or plant seeds as soon as they are ripe and keep them damp all winter in light soil. Germination will be in spring so plant out then and look forward to the flowers, which will appear in the third season. To stop the Kingcup from taking over it may be necessary to cull its numbers in autumn or give it some competition from a similar plant like Monkey Flower.

Pink Purslane. *Claytonia alsinoides.*
   Annual. Damp, rich soil.
When I first saw this I thought I had found something rather rare and, indeed, if I had been back in my native Midlands I would have been right, but in fact it is a fairly common plant of West and North Britain. It is hairless, growing about 30cm usually, and ending up as a spray of 15mm pink, five-petalled flowers, not unlike those of Campion.

The rounded, thick fleshy leaves give away the fact that it loves water or moist conditions. The name comes from the American botanist Clayton, though how he managed to get his name tagged to a very British species I am not sure – probably during the renaming of genuses.

Sow the 2.5 × 2.0mm ovoid black seeds thinly out of doors or in a cold frame in March and in damp compost and loam. Once they have reached a few centimetres they can be transplanted to a shady place in damp sandy peat and set about 30cm apart. Soil conditions are not as important as moisture. If you can manage Purslane then perhaps I can recommend the similar *Claytonia perfoliata* to test your mettle. It is an attractive, edible plant that does not like heavy soils.

Hemp Agrimony. *Eupatorium cannabinum.*
   Perennial. Damp soil.
If you are looking for an attractively coloured blaze of flowers then this will do pretty well because of the way that the small tubular flowers are clumped together in dense clusters of reddish mauve, white or purple. Wet ditches, damp, low lying land and woods, harbour this aromatic but bitter plant, which grows up to 2 metres (though usually it is only about 1 metre) from thick fleshy stock. Crowds of the plants can be seen flowering throughout the summer in coastal or low lying areas of England and Wales.

This 'cure for jaundice, coughs, catarrhs, and urinary obstructions' is pretty easy to get along with because it spreads fairly slowly and comes back year after year with a good show.

Planting should be between October and March when the plant is dormant and pretty small, into well drained soil in a sunny border. Division of roots in spring, cuttings of soft wood (recent growth) during summer and rooted in rich soil.

Seeds can be sown in spring in rich soil and under glass, and when are about 5cm tall transplanted where they are to flower.

Policeman's Helmet. *Impatiens glandulifera.*
Moist ground.
This is not a true British national plant because it was introduced to the nation in 1837 from its Himalayan homeland to be grown in the gardens of the gentry. It has not spread very far because the greatest concentrations can still be found in the North of England, but now there are enormous numbers lining streams, in marshy ground and in fact in most moist spots. From tough roots the simple stem grows up its 30–122cm giving off the broad serrated leaves, tinged with red at the nodes and carrying spiked 2cm pink lanterns that are the pretty, odd shaped flowers that appear from June to September. The flowering is not exactly prolific, but it does provide a nice show in quantity and it keeps going for a long time, producing the blooms that may be in fact any shade of pink between white and quite a deep red.

Amenable to being taken into the garden, the Policeman's Helmet is still grown like that in France and the Low Countries but the moisture of its soil must be kept up otherwise a wilt will set in.

Seeds can be sown out of doors in moist ground. Cuttings can be taken right the way through the summer, rooted in warm (75°F) sand and planted out that year. Transplant at anytime, though during flowering the prognosis is not as good because it is spending hard-earned energy on its blooms rather than its roots. Similarly, divide in autumn, the seed pods may 'explode' when touched, flinging seeds all over – so watch out!

Bog Asphodel. *Narthecium ossifragum.*
Perennial. Humus, acid, perhaps sphagnum soil.
For some odd reason it was thought to make the bones of cattle brittle and was hunted down accordingly, to be made (the berries) into a dye, which was later replaced by the imported saffron colouring. It has a tuft of very iris-shaped leaves and a 12cm flowering pedicel coming from the creeping rootstock. The stem is rather stiff and vertical with no hairs and the yellow flowers, which have tufts of white hairs on the anthers (about 15mm across), change colour in the autumn as they die off and leave a bright orange fruit. There is a sweetish scent and the seeds are about 1.5mm and oval white. It is found in upland areas of Scotland, West England and Wales, flowering in mid-summer.

Plant autumn or spring in ordinary or slightly peaty soil in a very moist place, dividing the roots at the same time. Seeds can be sown in a frame in moist peaty soil in April, put 1cm down, covered with a pane of glass to prevent losing moisture and planted out the following autumn. Alternatively the seeds can be sown out of doors, where the plant is to grow in April. Watch out for it spreading too fast.

Meadow-sweet. *Filipendula ulmaria.*
Perennial. Likes a non-acid soil.
A tall plant that everyone must have seen from the train at one time or

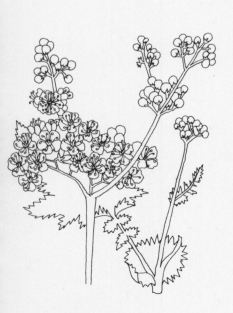

another and always wondered what it was, looking like a white flag in the green. Growing 120cm tall, with its erect, pinnate, leaved stem headed by an inflorescence of five-petalled flowers which are only about 5mm across each but all together make a thick, dense irregular blob about 7cm across. These flowers come out in June, July and August mainly, though they do linger on into September in some places and they have a rather sickly sweet smell which actually improves and becomes stronger after picking and ageing.

Found in meadows, swamps, fens, pond edges and the like in non acid soil throughout the British Isles, it was used as a distillate to strengthen the eyes and to flavour soups, for a long time.

So far the story of this flower must sound delightful, but I have some bad news, none of my gardening colleagues, nor I, nor reference texts, appear to know how exactly to grow it. There are a few vague things said like 'transplant in the autumn' but apart from this I shall just adapt the method from similar plants and this should be adequate. Seed is hardly ever developed, so its propagation by this means will prove difficult. Roots, however, are quite amenable to movement and division so I would suggest planting in either spring or autumn and division in autumn. It is very attractive so perhaps it will become common in our gardens.

As suggested above, a damp, alkaline soil is the best though it will easily tolerate the generally drier garden soil.

Lady's Smock or Milkmaid. *Cardamine pratensis.*
Perennial. Damp soil.
As a boy I used to live in a house which was lucky enough to have a field opposite it with a stream running through. The farmer didn't drain it very well and the cows kept to the grassier places so that left a few acres of rather infertile and damp ground in the field's centre. At the time I remember that the Milkmaid (that was the local name) grew up to my knees like the fog from horror films that whisps about the hero's boots.

Growing about 30cm high from the small fleshy tubers, it produces a small head of four petalled lilac flowers about 1cm across, which come out in succession from April to June. In fact there is a range of flower colour from a deep purple (pretty rare) to pure white all of which may be double in certain cases thus giving rise to varieties that were once common in the garden.

Flowering Rush. *Butomus umbellatus.*
Perennial. Likes ponds and water channels.
I'm not joking when I say that this makes a good garden plant that is easy to grow, because when it was taken to the USA to be grown in gardens, it escaped from this confinement to colonize huge parts of the St Lawrence. Growing up to three metres tall as a clump of slender leaves and a single flower stem from a thick rhizome and with fibrous roots, it produces a single umbel of flowers, which open one after the other all the way through June, July and August. The very striking pink, purple or white flowers grow about 2cm across each with a cluster of attractive stamens growing from the centre of the six-petalled cup. River margins, ponds and non-stagnant ditches seem to be its favourite hang outs but in Britain it is rather uncommon being found scattered in Central, Southern and Eastern England.

Plant it in April, before growth restarts, in boggy ground, rich wet soil or under 2cm of still water; divide the roots in spring.

Bladderworts

These are mildly pretty, brightly coloured plants that float on the surface of the water, anchored down by their roots and having little bladders on their leaves. They propagate most effectively by dropping bubils to the bottom of the pond and allowing them to grow. Therefore, I suggest transplanting a specimen in autumn and allowing it to 'self-seed', e.g. *Utricularia vulgaris*, the Greater Bladderwort.

Common Butterwort. *Pinguicula vulgaris.*

Perennial. Natural rich soil.

The Butterwort got its name because it was meant to be a protector of milk and butter yields as were many other flowers. Each plant produces a set of curious yellow and green leaves which have the property of being able to stick and digest flies and other insects. They are succulent to the touch, curl up at the edges to form a sort of trough and die away in winter. The flowers are held above the rest of the plant by 15cm stalks (there is usually more than one flower per plant), they are a deep purple and about 1cm across coming out in May, June, July and early August. Bogs, wet places, moist heaths and mountainous areas of Great Britain are its favourite hang outs.

In winter it retracts into itself as just a bud, with other buds forming offset bulbs round it and these can be separated off. Replanting of the bulbs can be done immediately in similar conditions to the original: a west or north-west facing place perhaps at the base of a slope to receive plenty of moisture. The soil should be porous but moisture retaining (slightly acid perhaps in the case of large flowered Butterwort), leaf mould mixed with sand would do, and it should be watered regularly because in the wild the Butterwort never allows itself to grow on a site that dries out.

Planting and division can be done in April. The state of the art with seeds is pretty refined; spring sowing of the minute seed in a cool frame in pots of a mixture of sphagnum moss, sand and standard compost. Water the seedlings more than you would anything else until they are large enough to be planted out in summer. The distribution of these plants around our islands tends to suggest that they like a warm climate, so protect them from frost, give them a sheltered station, but even then you may be unlucky because their culture is acknowledged to be hard.

Large-Flowered Butterwort. *Pinguicula grandiflora.*
    Perennial. Boggy ground.
A rare plant of South-West Ireland that is very similar to the common
variety except that it has a large (over 2cm) flower and is much more fussy
about its environment.
    You will have to be slightly more careful with its conditions than was
needed with *vulgaris* but it should grow all right. The main problem with
it is the acquisition of specimens originally which is admittedly hard,
though I'm sure a nurseryman will provide one.
    Culture is similar to that of the Common Butterwort.

Bristol Onion. *Allium sphaerocephalon.*
    Perennial. Calcareous soils.
Grows from a bulb in only one part of Britain (no prizes for guessing where)
with its 2cm head of purply flowers at the top of the 30–75cm stem which
is accompanied up by the hollow, round but long, pointed leaves.
    There are many forms of garlic in Britain but unfortunately most of
them are, like the Bristol Onion, very rare but they can all be grown in a
similar way by just changing the conditions to those of the plant in question.
    Plant the bulb in autumn or spring in well drained, light soil and in a
sunny position. They can be planted closely together for the greatest show,
but you will then have to lift and divide away the offsets rather more often
than the 3–4 years that is usually allowed (do this in August). If you like,
and this is not absolutely necessary, the bulbs can be lifted after dying
down. Vegetative reproductive methods are probably the most satisfactory because the black 3.0 × 3.5mm seeds, planted in late summer or spring
in the same soil, will not flower for three seasons. Bulbs will be bigger and
stronger for the following year if they are fed during flowering or slightly
after.

Ramsons. *Allium ursinum.*
    Perennial. Moist rich soil.
The plant likes damp, shady places, moist woods, moist hedges and meadows spread over the whole country (though concentrated in the western
wetter side). This member of the onion family grows in thick light green
clumps of twisted Lily-of-the-valley leaves and 45cm tall flowers. It grows
from a tuber and pushes up the leaves early in spring to follow them with
the triangular stem (smooth) bearing an umbel of six petalled, 5mm, white,
starry, flowers which form themselves into a ball about 4cm in diameter
from April to June. The oniony origins of the plant really makes itself felt:
the pungent, coarse, unpleasant odour that is issued fast at bruises in the
plant and slowly all over.
    Culture is similar to that of the Bristol Onion except that moister ground
is needed and this should be down wind of the house.

CHAPTER FIVE

Pure Enjoyment

I presume that everyone that has read this far will have grown the flowers –
I hope so! If not I hope you will.

Well, what has it all achieved? You have got a natural, more balanced,
British garden with all the things that entails, like less work, pretty flowers,
stronger plants, more wild life, a haven for birds and people. Packeted seeds,
expensive pesticides – unwanted, weed killers – unnecessary, it's a cheap
garden full of luxuries. Outside the back door there is a work of natural art,
closely intermingled, happily coexisting, beautifully decorative, a genuine
masterpiece of mother nature's wizardry (or is it witchcraft?). I hope that
now you've got the butterflies, birds, frogs and bees interested in YOUR
garden as somewhere worth going because there is actually a home there for
them now and food for them to eat. Let me expand on this just a little.

Some of the modern garden flowers often find themselves infested with
insects – earwigs find pure satisfaction in dahlias for instance – but it is certain
that natural British flowers harbour so many insects as to make a common
garden flower look useless. Instantly my mind flits to thoughts of gnats and
houseflies but really these will be no more problem now because they are
the ones that would have put up with foreign plants anyway. It is our
beauties, a development of years of evolution, that are the hardest hit by
exclusion of our national flowers. Butterflies have a definite flower, or small
range of them, on which to lay their eggs – if you don't have any Vetch in
your garden then you're just going to have to hope that next door's do
because you'll be missing a chance at about 10 different types of butterfly.
Can you actually say that you've seen a Brimstone? (which is the old name
for sulphur; they are bright yellow). They are common in the South East
of England, you may have seen one if you live in the country, but they need
leguminous plants, particularly clover or vetch on which to lay their eggs.
So this, the insect from which we probably get the word butterfly because
of its butter colour, is now unknown in the Metropolis, there being too few
of its favourite plants there. Nettles and long grass form an absolute sanc-
tuary for beautiful moths and butterflies but what do we do – chop them
down. Devil's bit scabious, rock rose, cow wheat, flowers needed for
certain species, what do we do with them? Leave them in the countryside
and forfeit the chance at butterfly time. Leave a little patch of your plot un-
touched, give it to the nettles or the long grass (studded with jewel buttercups if you like or subservient to a regal thistle) and you should see some
insect and perhaps butterfly results from it. Some of them will be short

lived, like the may-fly type which have their day and are gone. In France two years ago, at Louviers, I observed that over the days the insect population changed. On Monday the place swarmed with Common Blues, on Tuesday the Common Browns came to the foreground and on Wednesday it was the turn of the 'Cabbage White' (a term which covers a multitude of species). They used few pesticides on the farms at Louviers because the farmers are poor and this was the reason given to me by a French friend as to the amazing number of butterflies. Last summer in Denmark I saw mile after mile of fields where the hedging had been removed and replaced by wire fence. It was desolate – not a wild thing and what a waste, the farmer having sacrificed nature for his crops. If the no-pesticides-and-plenty-of-hedging way works in Europe to promote wild life then it will work here, so leave out the poisons. After all wild garden plants can look after themselves and birds will eat pests for you if given a chance.

You do like butterflies don't you? Perhaps the long lived ones will interest you the most; Small Tortoishell, Common Brimstone, and Red Admiral are particularly lucky in this direction, they may even live through the winter to limp around on battered wings in the New Year. The British Painted Lady has been recorded having flown to Iceland and many of our imports across the Channel live a considerable time, mate and give a young, English generation in the autumn. After mating the female flies off to find the flower that evolution has ordained her to lay eggs on. If it is not present then those eggs will be wasted. The Peacock and the Small Tortoishell lay in batches but they are exceptional in this respect, singles being the norm for the rest. After a few days – or months if it does, or has to, live through the winter – the ovum bursts and the caterpillar emerges to eat his way to maturity via coat after coat, only the head size staying roughly constant. They often have spines or are distasteful to deter the birds, a scheme which seems to allow them to get to the stage of pupation when they coat themselves in a hard metallic looking material and transform inside to the beautiful creature that emerges after a few weeks. Grab an oak branch in summer and shake it over a sheet of polythene, the insect life that falls out will probably stagger you, but mixed in will be the pupae of many butterflies. On page 118 is a list of the butterflies you have been doing down for so long in an ordinary flower garden, and with each one is guidance to its likes.

Other creatures are attracted too. Birds will go mad over a wild garden. Building materials for nests, the right insects to eat (with luck they should keep the creepy crawlies well in the background), seeds in the autumn, nesting places and the warmth of a well-kept compost heap. 'Weeds' improve the organic content of the soil and bring up minerals from the subsoil so the blackbird's swan-in-aspic, the worm, will be around in plenty. Just by giving them flowers they recognize, never mind the other benefits, the garden becomes a favourite haunt for birds of all types, so that not just the usual sparrows and starlings but perhaps a greenfinch or thrush might venture in. Birds form an integral part of an ecological system, they help to keep down the insects, so when each niche of the 'primary producer'

Wild Flowers for Butterflies

Butterfly name	Time when seen on the wing	Breeding flower
Silver Spotted Skipper	August	Bird's Foot Trefoil
Dingy Skipper	Late spring, early June	Bird's Foot Trefoil
Grizzled Skipper	Late spring, early June	Wild Strawberry
Checkered Skipper	May–June	Ground Ivy
Orange Tip (it is the male that has the tip)	Late spring	Milkmaid, Honesty
Brimstone	Spring and summer	Buckthorn
Clouded Yellow	Whole summer, early autumn	Leguminosae Clover, Mellilot
Green Veined White		Cruciferae (cabbage family) Milkmaid
Small White	May and late summer	
Large White		
Small Copper	Whole of summer	Dock and Sorrel
Large Blue	Rare	Thyme
Adonis Blue	June	Horseshoe Vetch
Holly Blue	May and August	Ivy, Holly
Swallowtail	June	Umbelliferous plants, Fennel, Parsley
Chalk Hill Blue	August and early September	Horseshoe Vetch
Common Blue	June and late August	Restharrow, Bird's Foot Trefoil
Small Blue	End May to Midsummer	Vetch
Silver Studded Blue	Late summer	Gorse, Broom, Heather
Brown Argus	May–June and August	Rockrose
White Admiral	July and early August	Woodland Honeysuckle
Red Admiral	Summer	Nettles
Comma	Summer	Nettles, Hop
Duke of Burgundy's Fritillary	June	Cowslip
Heath Fritillary	July	Cow Wheat
Marsh Fritillary	June	Devil's bit Scabious
Other Fritillaries	Summer, in West Country	Violets
Small Tortoishell	March till summer and August until hibernation	Nettles
Painted Lady	Homebred ones in August	Thistles
Peacock	May–June and July–late August	Nettles

plant habitat is filled there will be the tendency to fill up with the bird species that go with them. The goldfinch likes thistle seeds for instance. The family cat will just have to go by the board if birds are wanted in quantity, of course, because much as I like my feline friend she is bound to either put off or catch many of them. I'd just like to see her catch a bee.

Bees are foraging for nectar, their major source of energy, and pollen their main supplier of protein, when they explore the garden. Everyone has heard of the famous clover and heather honeys with their ever distinctive flavours, but really any plant that produces a copious volume of nectar will have the honour of producing honey indirectly. Dandelions, charlock, rosebay willowherb – perhaps these are the obscurer ones but they will make a bee happy. For pollen the bee need not look any further than the red deadnettle patch, the poppy bed, the colt's foot or the sow thistles, because they are all good producers. If you grow many flowers with the necessary properties then why don't you try introducing bees for sweet's sake?

Now, what has it achieved? A summer full of fluttering, entertaining, butterflies at least but is there anything else? History perhaps. By this I mean that those plants in your new garden have a millenia of habits, pastimes and folklore behind them. Under each plant in the list there are a few of the mystical uses it has and some of the lore about it but this isn't just plant archaeology – many uses still apply today.

SOME RECIPES

Dandelion wine, comfrey tea, nettle beer, rosemary conserve, rose butter, they might be 1000 years old but they still work fine. Here are just a few recipes:

Meadowsweet beer
Take 2 oz of meadowsweet, betony, agrimony and raspberry leaves, boil in 2 gallons of water for 20 minutes, strain and add 2 lb of sugar. Put this into a bucket and add some (not much will be needed) yeast, leave until fermentation stops (no bubbles rising to the surface copiously), add 1 tsp. of sugar to each of about 8 pint bottles, and fill them with the liquor. Two weeks later you'll have drinkable meadowsweet beer.

Ivy tea
Take about 10 fresh ground ivy leaves, wash them, put them into the teapot and pour over about $\frac{1}{2}$ a pot of boiling water, i.e. just make ground ivy tea the same way as ordinary tea – in fact add some of this if the taste is not strong enough for your liking.

Syrup of violets
Pick 1 pint of fresh violet (*Viola odorata*) flowers, pour over them (when washed) $2\frac{1}{2}$ pints of boiling water, leave a day, strain, add 3 lb. of sugar and stir into a syrup. Syrup of violets in fact.

Chicory flavouring
Chicory was the plant supposed to arise from the tears of the girl who cried for her sailor lover, whose ship never returned. It's a bitter herb. Put some in the stew and while you're there add some arrowhead leaves, brooklime, fennel or parsley.

Elderflower wine et al.
Take 2 pints of fresh elder flowers (you'd better have grown them yourself, mind!), boil them for 2 minutes in about $\frac{1}{2}$ gallon of water, leave

them to cool for 4 days, stirring occasionally, strain, add 2 lb. of white sugar and 2 pints of water stirring until dissolved. Add yeast, 1 tsp. of citric acid, some proprietary nutrient tablet for the yeast and leave to ferment open for a few days. Finish the fermentation in a closed airlocked jar, and bottle when fermentation has ceased and the wine almost clear. That recipe would have made wine from dandelions, cowslips, clover, rosepetals or meadowsweet.

Purple loosestrife tea

30–50 sun-dried grams of flower heads in a litre of boiling water for ten minutes gives a drink that is the remedy for many aliamentary ills. When in bloom bees will look at nothing else.

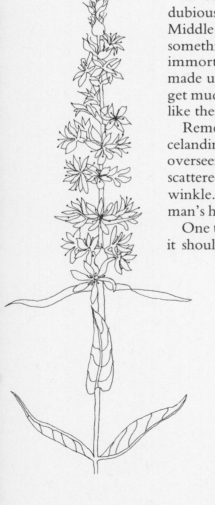

Rosemary, speedwell, betony and roses make good jams; coriander was used to flavour gin; pansies, bugloss, mellilot, borage, and roses make good cordials; ragwort and many others make a good dye; dandelions, jack-by-the-hedge, and willowherb make tasty salad greenery, and stitchwort makes a fine boiled vegetable.

In our plastic-coated, ultra-modern age the fumitory is considered a dubious remedy for freckles and elderberries that were planted widely in the Middle Ages to keep away evil spirits go unthought of. But doesn't it mean something that the simple tansy was given to Gannymede to make him immortal; and rather than a 'King's Ransom' hybrid tea rose, restharrow made up the crown of thorns Jesus wore to the Cross? How can you ever get much kick out of a plant that was invented last year when there are ones like these still around?

Remember the swathes of poppies in the long grass? Remember the celandines peeping out of the hedge in spring or the policeman's helmet overseeing the stream bank? Where are they now? Swathes of poppies scattered through the flower bed and poking their heads through the periwinkle. Celandines, starry eyed, glittering from the fence edge and policeman's helmet ruling a damp British corner just as it does in Belgian gardens.

One thing that impresses most is that it is all so much less work, or at least it should be; a peaceful harmony arising in a former place of siege. The weeds still come, but now they are flowery ones, self seeds from the flowers present rather than the eternal chickweed that presses up or groundsel that finds its way in. The garden has become a stage up the ecological succession, one rung up the ladder away from the weedy spreaders and the invasive grasses. Your wild flowers should control and dominate the garden at your command and they should pay good floral return in the process.

Now there is no excuse for not having flowers all over your garden, just because the garden varieties didn't fit. Now there is a fight for space on the hedge between clematis and hop, whereas before it might go unclothed. Now the wall is scattered with yellow and blue climbing wall ivies, the bog inhabited by asphodels, the lawn edge by daisies and the back border by mullein.

Every place in the garden provides a space for something wild and beautiful. All I can ask is that you fill those spaces.

A Plant Catalogue:
Choosing a Plant for the Job

Plants doing particularly well in full sun
ANNUALS: Field poppy 53, Cornflower 54, Corn Cockle 72, Pheasant's Eye 80, Flax 80.
BIENNIALS: Musk Mallow 43, Mulleins 44, Hound's Tongues 78, Scotch Thistle 84, Teasel 88.
PERENNIALS: Toadflaxes 45, Harebell 58, Heathers 60, Daisy 63, Thrift 64, Chicory 66, Chrysanthemums 67, Scabious 70, Common Bedstraw 73, Vetches 74, Buttercups generally 77, Yarrow 79, Common Fleabane 79, Ragwort 80, Sea Aster 81, Fumitory 82, Knapweeds 83, Cat's-foot 64, Thistles 84, Sea Holly 86, Elecampane 86, Hawkweeds 89, Hawkbits 89, Clovers 92, Snake's Head Fritillary 93, Stonecrops 95, Potentillas 96, Dog Rose 104, Cloudberry 102, Hop 105, Dyer's Greenweed 105, Small Bindweed 107, Monkeyflower 109, Policeman's Helmet 112, Lady's Smock 113.

Plants doing particularly well in the shade
ALL PERENNIALS: Primrose 43, Cowslip 44, Oxslip 44, Wood Forget-me-not 46, Herb Robert 47, Hairy St John's Wort 56, Bluebell 56, Wood Sorrel 66, Some Bistorts 65, Wintergreens 66, Comfrey 71, Lesser Celandine 76, Goldilocks 77, Archangel 90, White Deadnettle 90, Orpine 95, Yellow Pimpernel 102, Creeping Jenny 103, Yellow Loosestrife 110, Ramsons 115.

Coastal plants or those particularly found towards the coast
ANNUAL: Common Centaury 87.
BIENNIAL: Yellow Horned Poppy 52.
PERENNIALS: Bloody Cranesbill 47, Sea Campion 50, Nottingham Catchfly 50, Sea Lavender 62, Thrift 64, Corn Marigold 68, Scabious 70, Sea Aster 81, Sea Holly 86.

Notably climbing plants
PERENNIALS: Melilot 75, Stitchwort 81, Fumitories 82, Ivy Leaved Toadflax 99, Honeysuckle 102, Roses 104, Hop 105, Bindweed 107.

Plants hardly ever found on chalky or limey ground
ANNUALS: White Climbing Fumitory 82.
BIENNIALS: Foxglove 41.
PERENNIALS: Wood Forget-me-not 45, Dusky Cranesbill 48, Marsh Violet 54, Common and Slender St John's wort 55, Bluebell 56, Heathers 59,

Common Meadow Rue 63, Wood Sorrel 66, Wintergreens 66, Corn Marigold 68, Devil's Bit Scabious 70, Fragrant Agrimony 68, Marsh Ragwort 80, Tormentil 97, Trailing Tormentil 97, Broom 106, Gorses 106, Kingcup 110, Butterworts 114.

Plants usually found on chalky or basic ground
ANNUALS: Yellow Wort 64, Pheasant's Eye 80.
BIENNIALS: Mulleins 44.
PERENNIALS: Cowslip 44, Bloddy Cranesbill 47, Meadow Cranesbill 47, Meadow Saffron 51, Mountain Pansy 53, Clustered Bellflower 58, Gladdon 60, Common Valerian 61, Chicory 66, Common Milkwort 67, Small Scabious 70, Hedge Bedstraw 73, Crosswort 73, Northern Bedstraw 74, Some Vetches 74, Greater Knapweed 83, Rough Hawkbit 89, Common Spotted Orchis 93, Shrubby Cinquefoil 97, Mountain Avens 99, Wild Thyme 100, Sweet Briar 104, Meadow Sweet 112, Bristol Onion 115.

Tall plants often over one metre tall
ANNUALS: Corn Cockle 72.
BIENNIALS: Foxglove 42, Common Mallow 42, Mulleins 44, Field Scabious 69, Hound's Tongues 78, Teasel 88.
PERENNIALS: Common Mallow 42, Larger Cranesbills 48, Nettle Leaved Bellflower 58, Common Valerian 61, Common Meadow Rue 63, Field Scabious 69, Comfrey 71, Ragwort 80, Sea Aster 81, Thistles 84, Elecampane 86, Rosebay Willowherb 86, Great Hairy Willowherb 87, Honeysuckle 102, Roses 104, Hop 105, Broom 106, Gorse 106, Small and Greater Bindweed 107, Hemp Agrimony 111, Policeman's Helmet 112, Meadow Sweet 112, Flowering Rush 113.

Short plants usually less than 20cm tall
ANNUALS: Forget-me-nots 46, Field Speedwell 101, Scarlet Pimpernel 102.
PERENNIALS: Toadflaxes 45, Water Forget-me-nots 46, Wood Forget-me-nots 46, Crocuses 51, Violets 53, Bluebell 56, Harebell 58, Heathers 59, Daisy 63, Thrist 64, Cat's-foot 64, Wood Sorrel 66, Common Milkwort 67, Bugle 71, Lesser Celandine 76, Coltsfoot 83, Clovers 92, Stonecrops 95, Potentillas 96, Mountain Avens 99, Wild Thyme 100, Germander Speedwell 101, Yellow Pimpernel 102, Creeping Jenny 102.

Particularly late-flowering plants often extending after mid September
ANNUALS, Speedwells 101, Common Centaury 87, some Vetches 74.
PERENNIALS: Crocuses 51, Daisy 63, Chicory 66, Chrysanthemums 67, Devil's Bit Scabious 70, Sea Aster 81, Vetches 74, Turkscap lily 93, Hawksbits and Hawkweeds 89, Dandelion 91, Periwinkle 55.

Particularly early-flowering plants often coming into bloom before mid April
ANNUALS: Field Speedwell 101.
PERENNIALS: Primulacaea 44, Violets 53, Bluebell 58, Bell Heather 60, Gorse

106, Irish Heath 59, Daisy 63, Crosswort 73, Lesser Celandine 76, Goldilocks 77, Stitchwort 81, Colt's Foot 83, Barstard Balm 85, Early Purple Orchis 93, Wood Anemone 61, Pasque Flower 51.

Water plants or those that thrive in damp conditions
ANNUAL: Pink Pruslane 111.
PERENNIALS: Water Forget-me-not 46, Marsh or Bog Violet 53, Gladdon 60, Grass of Parnassus 65, Bistorts 65, Devil's Bit Scabious 70, Lesser Celandine 76, Spearworts 77, Sneezewort 79, Marsh Ragwort 80, Great Hairy Willowherb 87, Water Mint 91, Snake's Head Fritillary 93, Early Purple Orchis 93, Common Spotted Orchis 93, Marsh Cinquefoil 98, Creeping Jenny 101, Bog Pimpernel 102, Yellow Waterlily 108, White Waterlily 108, Yellow Flag 109, Monkey Flower 109, Arrowhead 109, Yellow Loosestrife 110, Kingcup 110, Hemp Agrimony 111, Policeman's Helmet 112, Bog Asphodel 112, Milkmaid or Lady's Smock 113, Flowering Rush 113, Bladderworts 114, Ramsons 115.

Rockery Plants
PERENNIALS: Bladder and Sea Campion 50, Periwinkle 55, Heathers 59, Herb Bennet 61, Thrift 64, Bedstraws 73, some Vetches 74, Yarrow 79, all Stonecrops 95, Potentillas 96, Mountain Avens 99.

Plants not mentioned in any of the other lists that are not extreme in their demands or stature
ANNUALS: Campions Red and White 49, Borage 71.
BIENNIALS: Spreading Bellflowers 57, Viper's Bugloss 72.
PERENNIALS: Ragged Robin 49, Anemone Pulsillata 51, Welsh poppy 52, Periwinkles 55, Globe flower 57, many Bellflowers 57, Greater Celandine 64, Feverfew 68, Tansy 68, Agrimony 70, Yarrow 79, White Horehound 85, Meadow Goat's Beard 88, Hawkweeds 89, and many Hawkbits 89, Mint 91, Woad 92, Round-leaved Fluellen 100 and Sharp-leaved Fluellen 100, many of the cabbage family 92.

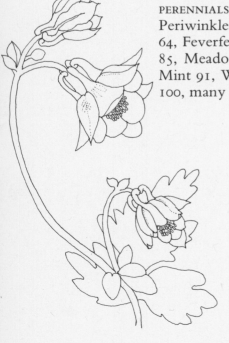

APPENDIX II

Conservation of Wild Creatures and Wild Plants Act 1975

This is what we have been waiting for for too long. There have been false starts, changes in sponsors, too few readings in the House, changes of Government which have added together to get this legislation onto the Statute Book behind most other European countries.

The attention of Parliament was drawn to it by a determined group of M.P.s headed by the Right Honourable Peter Hardy, one of its main sponsors. It is certainly not ahead of its time that it should have been adopted now, for we have more species endangered by man's callous disregard than ever before.

All of the Act is important to nature lovers but the clauses that affect us, as would-be wild flower gardeners, are the following sections:

4.   If, save as may be permitted by or under this Act, any person, other than an authorised person, without reasonable excuse uproots any plant, he shall be guilty of an offence.

5.   If, save as may be permitted by or under this Act, any person without reasonable excuse picks, uproots or destroys any protected plant, he shall be guilty of an offence unless the picking, uprooting or destruction occurs as an accidental result, which could not reasonably have been avoided, of any operation which was carried out in accordance with good agricultural or forestry practice.

7.   Says that the Secretary of State can vary the Schedule of plants involved and the way they are affected.

8.   Says that licences are required to contravene the Act. These are not generally supplied for gardening purposes and are given by the Nature Conservancy Council in most cases. The licences may be revoked or changed after issue.

9.10.11.   These deal with the enforcement, with punishment of offenders or suspected offenders. Fines up to £100 per species can be imposed.

14.   This section states that Schedule change will be printed in The London and Edinburgh Gazette.

15.   Defines a few terms and 'pick' in relation to plants means gather or pluck, but not uproot, any part of the plant from the land on which it is growing.
     'Plant' means, subject to subsection (2) (which says that fungi and alga are not included in the Act, whereas lichens are) of the

section, any plant growing wild on any land.

'Protected plant' means a plant specified in Schedule (2) of this Act.

'Uproot' in relation to a plant means pull up, dig up, or remove the plant with its root from the land on which it is growing.

'Authorised person' means the owner or occupier, or any servant of the owner or occupier, or any person authorised by the owner or occupier of the land on which the plant is growing.

17.   (2) This Act shall not extend to Northern Ireland.

I have not quoted the whole Act here and it would be advisable for you to get a copy yourself. It costs 20p. from Her Majesty's Stationery Office.

In the Act itself, Schedule 2 includes:

Species of Protected Plants.

Common Name	Scientific Name
Alpine Gentian	Gentiana nivalis
Alpine Sow-thistle	Cicerbita alpina
Alpine Woodsia	Woodsia alpina
Blue Heath	Phyllodoce caerulea
Cheddar Pink	Dianthus gratianopolitanus
Diapensia	Diapensia lapponica
Drooping Saxifrage	Saxifraga cernua
Ghost Orchid	Epipogium aphyllum
Killarney Fern	Trichomanes speciosum
Lady's-slipper	Cyprepedium calceolus
Mezereon	Daphne mezereum
Military Orchid	Orchis militaris
Monkey Orchid	Orchis simia
Oblong Woodsia	Woodsia ilvensis
Red Helleborine	Cephalanthera rubra
Snowdon Lily	Lloydia serotina
Spiked Speedwell	Veronica spicata
Spring Gentian	Gentiana verna
Teesdale Sandwort	Minuartia stricta
Tufted Saxifrage	Saxifraga caespitosa
Wild Gladiolus	Gladiolus illyricus

Remember that once every five years at least the Nature Conservancy Council will review the Schedule so that it will change and that it is illegal to take a plant without the permission of the landowner.

Wild flower seeds available commercially

The greatest variety of supply seems to come from Thompson & Morgan (Ipswich) Ltd, who have two grades of supply:

Easily available seed of

Armeria maritima
Atropa belladona
Bellis perennis (varieties only)
Calluna vulgaris
Campanula rotundifolia
Centaurea cyanus, moshata
Digitalis purpurea
Dryas octopetala
Fritillaria mileagaris
Humulus lupulus
Iris foetidissima
Isatis tinctoria
Centranthus ruber

Lilium martagon
Primula elatior
Primula officinalis
Primula farinosa
Primula vulgaris
Anemone pulsatilla
Rosa canina
Sedum acre
Statice limonium
Thymus vulgaris
Trollius europaeus
Veronica spicata

Smaller quantities available of

Adonis aestivalis
Anthyllis vulneraria
Chelidonium majus
Corydalis lutea
Lonicera periclymenum
Lychnis flos-cuculi

Meconopsis cambrica
Papaver rhoeas
Parnassia palustris
Polygonum bistorta
Verbascum thapsus

Bulk seed mixtures are available from: Nickerson's, Field House, Grimsby, Lincs.

Botanical Society of the British Isles' Code of Conduct

Observe the law

It is now illegal for anyone, without permission of the owner or occupier, to dig up any wild plant

A small number of very rare plants in danger of extinction (21 in 1975) are totally protected by law, and removal of *any* part of these plants is an offence

DO NOT dig up wild plants without permission

DO NOT dig up or pick any protected plant

PICK ONLY FLOWERS KNOWN TO BE COMMON OR PLENTIFUL IN THE LOCALITY, BUT WHENEVER YOU CAN LEAVE THEM FOR OTHERS TO ENJOY

If you wish to identify a plant take the smallest adequate bit. Often a sketch or photograph may serve the purpose. If living plants are needed for cultivation take seed or cuttings sparingly and never from rare or protected plants.

Safeguard the habitat

For convervation of our wild plants the first essential is to preserve the sort of place and conditions they can grow in. *This can easily and unwittingly be damaged by people*. Watch your step. Treading compacts the soil preventing seeding establishment and breaking off young shoots.

When you visit a rare plant, avoid doing anything which would expose it to unwelcome attention, such as making an obvious path to it or trampling on the vegetation round it.

'Gardening' before taking photographs may also give away the site. Bear in mind too how readily nearby plants can be crushed by the toes of kneeling photographers.

Remember that photographs themselves can give clues to the localities of rare plants, quite apart from the information accompanying them.

Avoid telling people about the site of a plant you believe to be rare. Your local nature conservation trust should, however, be informed, which will help safeguard it.

Respect requests from conservation bodies or land owners not to visit particular sites at certain times.

Teachers and leaders of outings and field meetings are particularly urged to bear these points in mind.

Avoid thoughtless introductions

Plants should not be introduced into the countryside without the knowledge and agreement of your local natural conservation Trust, or of the Botanical Society of the British Isles, c/o Dept. of Botany, British Museum (Nat. Hist.), Cromwell Road, London, sw7 5BD.

Glossary

Achene   Loosely it is a small capsule containing a seed that is shed from the plant for distribution.

Anther   This is the male, pollen-bearing part of the flower.

Axil   The angle between the leaf and its parent stem.

Basal   Low down – basal leaves are those closest to the earth for instance.

Climax vegetation   The population of plants in a particular place where the forces for the change of that population all oppose each other.

Decumbent   Low, horizontal, earth-hugging.

Ecological niche   A situation in the environment that, through its content of special quantities of plant necessities specifies, as a lock specifies the key, the plant that best fits the situation.

Ecology   The study of the interactions between organisms and their environment.

Ecosystem   The entire group of organisms that interact with each other to use nature's resources in the most economical manner and set apart from other such groups.

Floret   A small flower that makes up part of one bigger one; e.g. the small, yellow disc florets that make up the centre of the daisy's flower.

Fusiform   Broad in the middle and tapering towards either end.

Homeostasis   The tendency of biological systems once mature to resist change.

Inflorescence   An entire group of flowers that are together on a plant.

Lanceolate   Much thinner than long and tapering slowly towards the end.

Leguminous   This means an ability to synthesize nitrogen fertilisers from the air, using bacteria in the roots.

Mucilaginous   Having the properties of mucilage; i.e. viscous, moist, sticky.

Nodes   The points on a stem from which leaves or flowers spring.

Palmate   Shaped like a palm where many ribs in the leaf blade meet together and from that common point the petiole goes to meet the stem.

Pappus   A downy or bristly attachment to a seed or achene generally used to help distribute the seeds.

Pedicel   Minor stalks bearing flowers.

Pellucid dots   Clear, translucent dots on a leaf surface.

Perennation   The business of surviving until the next year.

Petiole   The part of a leaf that joins the blade to the stem.

Pinnate   Where the petiole gives rise to only one main rib to a leaf.

Raceme   An inflorescence in which the flowers are equal distances apart and on short pedicels from a common stem; e.g. Agrimony.

Rhizome   A swollen underground stem that produces roots and is often used for perenation.

Sepals   The normally uninteresting covers for the unopened flower that remain external to the petals during bloom.

Stamens   The anther plus the filament – the stalk the anther is on.

Stolon   A prostrate or reclining shoot that will root and produce aerial growth at its nodes.

Stoloniferous   With or like stolons.

Style   The chanel in the female flower down which the pollen grows to fertilise the ovum.

Testa   The hard seed coating.

Vegetative reproduction   Production of new plants identical to the parent genetically and thus not including sexual reproduction.

Plant Index

Index to Latin Names

Hedgehog Grass

Daisy

Black
Byrony

Fleaba

milfoil

Field
Scabious

Ploughmans
Spikenyard

Bird's Foot
Trefoil

Greater Celandine
Shepherd's Needle